The Pilgrim's Tale

To Donald
with thanks & best
wishes,

Margaret.

The Pilgrim's Tale
One Hundred Days Of Hope
Margaret Keltie

Shoving Leopard

First published in 2010 by
Shoving Leopard
Flat 2F3, 8 Edina Street
Edinburgh
EH7 5PN
United Kingdom
http://www.shovingleopard.com/

The publishers gratefully acknowledge permission to reproduce the
following extracts in the text. We shall be delighted to rectify any
omissions, where we have been unable to identify a source, upon
application via email.
Chapter 2: 'Desert Christians' by Paulinus, Bishop of Nola translated
by Helen Waddell in 'Medieval Latin Lyrics' Penguin Classics 1952
Chapter 8: 'Gin I was God' Charles Murray (the Pig Poet 1864-1941)
public domain – but to be found in Hamewith – the Collected Poems
of Charles Murray, edited by Colin Milton, Aberdeen University Press
1979
Chapter 10: 'God has called you; he will not fail you' by Diane Davis,
copyright 1971. The Fishermen, Inc. from 'Sound of Living Waters'
Hodder and Stoughton

ISBN 978 1 905565 17 7

A catalogue record for this book is available from the British
Library.

Dedicated to the memory of
the five members of one family
who died in the storm on South Uist
on 11th January 2005:
Calum Campbell,
Archie, Murdina, Andrew and Hannah Macpherson.

'Since Jesus died and broke loose from the grave, God will most certainly bring back to life those who died in Jesus.'
(1 Thessalonians 4: 14 *The Message*)

A Word of Thanks

A good number of people have had a substantial input into this study and it is only right that their contribution should be fully acknowledged and appreciated.

The original motivation to write came from Janet de Vigne's inspirational title, which suggested so much about life's journey that I wanted to share.

Many others have agreed to allow parts of their own stories to be told as examples of the 'unbreakable hope' that is the subject of the study. Some names have been changed to preserve confidentiality, but I should like to record profound thanks to everyone who was willing to tell me — or to let me recount — their hope-filled experiences.

Editorial and critical input of an extremely substantial and encouraging nature has been given to me by my sister, Jean Keltie, and my friend, Jackie Baldwin. Both their theological training and their life experiences have made them invaluable supporters. I could not have completed the work without their faithful feedback and wise contributions.

Finally, especial thanks are due to my friend, Eleanor Muir, who provided the study space, time and encouragement to allow me to do the work.

Contents

Introduction

Hope is surely one of our most vital attributes, not only for survival in life, but also for a sense of purpose and direction. Those who have hope may have real trials to face, but they seem to come through them more successfully than those without it. Conversely, someone who seems to have everything going for him or her, yet has no hope, may feel life is not worth living. An attribute that can transform our experience so totally, truly deserves our close attention, and this study may provide an opportunity to discover more about the nature of that transformative hope which gives us mettle for troubled times and purpose for good times.

It is however a study rather than a rapid read, and although you may like to skim through it to gain a general impression of the direction taken, you will probably find it more beneficial to take it section by section, as the title suggests, and allow time for the reflection suggested at the end of each section. This could be done individually or in a group study. There are ten chapters with ten sections in each, with a task or question at the end of each section. If a group study is being undertaken, perhaps a chapter at a time would be more appropriate, with each member bringing his or her own reflections on each section back to the group.

Whichever way you decide to read it, may your study turn out to be invigorating and enabling, stimulating life-giving hope in you as an individual and/or in the group you belong to.

One further point worth making at this introductory stage is that although my perspective is a Christian one, I do not want to assume that everyone reading this study has the same perspective. The subject should be open to consideration by everyone, as the need for hope is universal. An examination of the specifically Christian hope will form the major part of the study, but that should not preclude fruitful discussion with those of other faiths or none, as we all seek to make sense of our shared life in this world.

Chapter 1: Plotting the Journey

Section 1

At the start of our study of the widely appealing concept of 'hope', it may be helpful to clarify what kind of hope we are considering. In some ways, it is easier to determine first what is *not* being considered. Hope, for example, can be used to mean something we wish for but have no certainty about. I may say as you set out on holiday:

'I hope you have a good time',

without intending the remark to have any guarantees attached that you will in fact enjoy yourself. I could say about the flight you are catching:

'I hope it will not be too late for you to make the connecting flight', but I have no certainty about it. I am simply expressing a wish. If you fall ill on your holiday, I may send you a card saying:

'I hope you feel better soon',

although I cannot say for sure that you will. I am simply expressing goodwill. Such wishes can show solidarity with our friends. However, this is not the sort of hope I propose to consider in this study.

Another common way in which 'hope' is used is to describe someone's temperament. For example, I may say:

'Jennifer is a very hopeful person',

meaning that she has an optimistic outlook or even that she has been fortunate in life and therefore expects things to go well. Again, this is a legitimate usage, but not the one I wish to consider in this study.

Rather I want to examine the hope described in the New Testament book of Hebrews, which is a letter written by a Christian author of the first century to a group of Jewish Christians. In chapter 6, verses 19-20, he says:

> 'We who have run for our very lives to God have every reason to grab the promised hope with both hands and never let go. **It's an unbreakable spiritual lifeline**, reaching past all appearances right to the very presence of God where Jesus, running on ahead of us, has taken up his permanent post as high priest for us' (*The Message* version of the Bible, translated by Eugene Peterson; bold letters mine.)

For those who accept that the Bible is a generally authoritative source, this hope is not therefore a weak ineffectual wishing but is based on a longstanding promise of blessing and peace which the God of the Bible has made to his people and through them to the whole world. This hope is guaranteed by the entrance of Jesus Christ into the presence of God after he rose from death. If 'the presence of God' is an alien concept to you, it may be helpful to think of it as a conviction that, despite all evidence to the contrary, the deepest reality is both benign and personal and that one can live in complete harmony with that person, in both this life and the next.

The importance of knowing what kind of hope we are talking about lies partly in the fact that we can do ourselves and others a great deal of harm if we misinterpret the true nature of this 'unbreakable' hope. We could, for example, expect things which God has not promised and place our hope mistakenly in thoughtless or over-optimistic predictions about this life which can only crumble in the face of reality.

Part of this study will be an attempt to establish what unbreakable hope does actually offer us, and set out a sound basis for that hope so that we may build on rock and not on sand.

1. Task/ Question (By yourself)
Can you think of a falsely optimistic hope that has caused you, or someone you know, grief in the past? What would have been a more realistic expectation?

*

Section 2

Having cleared away some ordinary uses of the word 'hope', we are in a position to ask in more detail what the 'unbreakable hope' — as I shall call it hereafter — consists of. It is possible that some readers may find that this and the following section contain material that seems unfamiliar or even unintelligible. If so, I would urge you to skim through them on a first reading and return to study them later if you feel the need, when you have 'got your ear in' for this substantial subject. In the meantime, take up the detailed reading at the last paragraph of Section 3.

Although not everyone reading this study may believe in the authority of the Bible, its teachings on hope are certainly worth exploring and many of them do posit a kind of hope that turns our usual way of thinking upside down. The passage already quoted from Hebrews is one of these. The imagery used in most versions of this passage is that of hope being an anchor in the presence of God, and the characteristic of this anchor most emphasised is its strength and security.

This anchor in wholeness and reality is one that is desperately needed by a world estranged from its true self, where individuals experience a sense of alienation and dislocation from themselves, one another and God. Relying on this anchor is a way of holding on to the instinct we have that life could and should be much more wholesome than it often appears.

The reason given for the certainty of this hope is that Jesus Christ — the one whom Christians believe to be specially chosen and sent by God as his representative to bring wholeness to the world — is now in God's presence, despite having been alienated and estranged from God himself by having had all the sins of the world heaped upon him as the Bible expresses it. This however did not prevent him from returning to be with God and so this is an assurance that we ourselves — however ill qualified we may feel ourselves to be — may be with God too if we come there as those who are aligned with Christ.

This assurance is certain because it does not depend on our own success as human beings, something which is always going to be — at the very least — questionable. The certainty of this hope depends on the character of God himself as shown in the goodness of Christ who, by rising from death, showed himself to be more powerful than the forces of alienation and dislocation which sought to destroy him. This then opens a way into God's presence for those who would otherwise have no right to be there.

Another passage, from the New Testament letter to the Christians in Rome, expands on this unbreakable hope by showing how it affects us in our daily lives. The experience of the presence of God throws a completely new light on our lives.

> 'We rejoice in the hope of the glory of God. Not only so, but we also rejoice in our sufferings, because we know that suffering produces perseverance; perseverance, character; and character, hope. And hope does not disappoint us, because God has poured out his love into our hearts by the Holy Spirit, whom he has given us. (Romans 5:2b-5 *New International Version* of the Bible)

At this point we come across one of the paradoxes inherent in the whole issue of unbreakable hope — that it is both a present reality and a future expectation. The extract begins with rejoicing in a present reality and goes on to describe a process that has still to be completed: the movement from suffering to hope. In the more usual way of thinking we would pass from suffering to despair, but this passage insists on the opposite: that suffering leads to hope.

2. Task/Question (to be undertaken by a group)

Look at the progression from suffering to hope in this passage and work out how that transition is made. Bear in mind that we are thinking about **unbreakable** hope — not merely a weak sort of wishing.

*

Section 3

The last part of the passage in Romans declares that character produces hope. It then goes on to claim that the reason why the sort of hope produced by character never disappoints us is that such character — such moral strength and spiritual integrity — has been developed in us by the action of God, described here as the Holy Spirit. It is secure because it is something God himself has achieved in our minds and hearts.

If such thinking seems very foreign, it is because we are so accustomed to being in charge of our own lives and setting our own aims and objectives. Coming into the presence of God may seem very far from the focus of our hope. We may have our sights set on all sorts of more mundane issues, such as getting through a difficult day at work or building a house or passing an exam or recovering from an illness — all perfectly natural objectives and ones which we can sometimes achieve and which God may delight to bring about in answer to prayer.

Yet the passage in Romans suggests that the actual processes we go through as we try to achieve any target may be more important than the achieving or otherwise of that target. These processes may shape us into strong, determined, courageous people who learn to look beyond the immediate objective and discover that we can survive all sorts of setbacks. Far from annihilating us, as we fear, these setbacks show the difference between, on the one hand, the achieving of some particular outcome and, on the other, the calibre of the thinking, feeling, creative, responsive person who is engaged with the issue, whatever it may be. In other words, the experiences we go through may in fact be used by God himself to realise an ambition which *he* has for us. Anyone who has had many dealings with God will recognise that the outcome is often very different to the one he or she envisaged, and that it gives an exciting sense of being part of a higher and more all-embracing purpose than his or her own.

A possible way of learning how to follow and develop this path of unbreakable hope is to use as a starting point a verse in 1 John 1:5b:

'God is light; in him there is no darkness at all' (*NIV*)

This is another way of saying that God is altogether good and there is nothing bad in him whatsoever. It is a resounding endorsement of the character of God as the foundation of all unbreakable hope.

3. Task/Question (By yourself)
While you are doing this study you might like to conduct an experiment. Try using the statement from 1 John as your non-negotiable starting point in every issue; 'God is light; in him there is no darkness at all'. So if, for example, you are wondering why terrible tragedies happen, such as the tsunami on Boxing Day 2004, or on a more personal level why some aspect of your own life is difficult, whatever answer you come up with, it would exclude an indifferent or cruel or powerless God of the universe, because 'in him there is no darkness at all.'

*

Section 4

A Personal Experience:
While I was writing the first draft of this study of hope, I was making a slow recovery from a painful back condition, caused by a protruding disc which was pressing on the sciatic nerve and so also causing a painful right leg. It lasted for about ten months and came in two phases, the second being much more severe than the first. My thoughts and feelings connected with this experience gave me a way of working out in practice some of the issues connected with hope.

The first few days of immobilisation were a nuisance but not a great trial. What was much harder to take was the next five months of nagging — though not excruciating — pain. I prayed for healing myself and asked others to pray for me too, which they faithfully did. The pain did not go away but neither did I fall into discouragement or depression, which I was tempted to do. I remembered texts such as:

> 'All things work together for good to them that love God' (Romans 8:28, *King James Version* of the Bible)

and assumed there must be a purpose. I certainly had never previously been so committed to daily walking, which eased the pain before it became more severe.

Medically, I entered the long-drawn-out process of being referred to an orthopaedic surgeon, who then referred me for an MRI scan. The results of this took me back to the orthopaedic surgeon and then to a neurosurgeon. It can be told in a sentence but there was a long wait between each one, only relieved by sporadic and rather inconclusive visits to a physiotherapist.

The second and more severe attack meant I was off work for five weeks, during which time I was immobilised, having to be waited on hand and foot by my longsuffering family while taking strong painkillers. Again I and others prayed daily, and as before, the pain did not go away. Yet the discouragement and weariness that go with such a condition were successfully banished, which I was very relieved about, as this time walking was too painful and so I was cooped up inside for weeks.

I had heard that this sort of back trouble could be very persistent, or at least, recurring, and so I knew the prognosis might not be too good for me. Others said that with a positive attitude and a willingness to do the exercises, the outlook was promising. The point I had to grapple with was that I might have to live with chronic pain and how would the unbreakable hope of the Bible sustain me in such a situation? A verse which seemed to offer practical wisdom was Proverbs 21:31:

> 'Do your best, prepare for the worst —
> Then trust God to bring victory.' (*The Message*)

What I like about this verse is that there is no suggestion that we should make our hope in God conditional on his fulfilling our own wishes — no attempt to bargain or manipulate. There is however an expectant looking to him and a reliance on his good purposes.

What happened was that in the few days after finishing the first draft of the account of my sore back, I experienced a decreasing of pain and was able to stop taking painkillers altogether. The neurosurgeon's appointment came round at this point and I was told that I did not need an operation as things stood. This — I need hardly say — was very wonderful to me and led me to conclude that there was a connection in God's purposes between my experience and the writing of this study.

4. Task/Question (By yourself)

Think of something in your own situation which might be a suitable subject about which to exercise hope. Give a vocal or written account of it — the facts, your thoughts and feelings about it and how you think God might be using it. You might want to share this with a trusted friend. Bear in mind that the purposes of God are of course sometimes mysterious to us for long periods of time and it may be necessary to rest on the truth that whatever is happening, 'God is light; in him there is no darkness at all.'

*

Section 5

The experience I have outlined above raises one of the key questions about unbreakable hope: what is the connection between it and our more ordinary hopes for our day-to-day lives? It may be helpful to consider a comparison with parents' hopes for their children. These might centre round their children growing up to become decent men and women, honest, hardworking, compassionate people who make a real difference in the world. Some such desire will motivate parents to undertake the detailed training, discipline, encouragement and love which children need as they grow up.

However, as this process continues from day to day, the children themselves will have distinctive desires and hopes of their own, as well as characteristics and aptitudes which emerge increasingly and which become part of the equation. The dynamic between parents and children will incorporate a daily negotiation and ideally an eventual harmony between the purposes of both parties. Generally speaking, the strong love which most parents have for their own offspring and the dependence which the young have upon their parents mean that this process happens successfully enough to ensure an adequate degree of maturity in the offspring, as well as a continuing relationship between the generations.

The average parent will refuse a dangerous request of the child's, but will consider the merits of other requests. Will granting the request cause the child to become spoiled? Will it cause pain to a third party? Does the child need a break or some encouragement? Can the parent afford it? Is there enough time? Should it be granted now or at a later date? Most parents enjoy giving their children a good time and so will only refuse if they need to; and if the children are old enough to understand, they will be given the reason. Most children will learn eventually that they cannot have everything they want when they want it, and become reasonably cooperative with their parents, internalising the decision-making processes for themselves.

Of course, this parent/child relationship can either fail to be properly established in the first place or break down irretrievably, and when either happens, it causes many of the social problems and much of the human misery of our society. Nevertheless, we all have a notion of how we think the relationship should work and it is that relationship which can shed light on the connection between unbreakable hope and ordinary hope.

The unbreakable hope is like the certainty in the children of their parents' love towards them and good aspirations for them. This certainty is what enables the child to accept the refusal of, or delay in granting, any particular request. The particular request would, of course, be like one of our ordinary hopes. This experience we have of the parent/child relationship is a reflection of the spiritual reality of the fatherhood of God, who, according to the Bible, desires us to be born into his family and develop as his sons and daughters.

5. Task/Question (By yourself)

Think of a clash of purpose with your own parents, or one between you and your children. Tell, in written or spoken form, what the issues were and how it was resolved — whether satisfactorily or otherwise.

*

Section 6

If we are, or would like to be, God's children (see John 1:12) as well as his creation, we need to have that certainty of his love and good purposes towards us, so that we can receive the experiences of life filtered through that certainty and in no other way. I would like to return therefore to the essential connection between hope and character, our own character, but more especially that of God himself, in whose nature there is no darkness at all. How can we find out about God's nature so that we may build that unbreakable hope upon it? Again, if you are unsure about the authority of the Bible, I would ask you to suspend disbelief for the purposes of exploration.

A place to begin would be in God's own introduction of himself to his people just as they were in the process of being formed into his people.

> 'I am the Lord your God, who brought you out of Egypt, out of the land of slavery. You shall have no other gods before me.'
> (Exodus 20:2-3 *NIV*)

It is interesting that God identifies himself primarily here as one who sets them free, one who brings them out of the place of slavery. For the ancient Hebrews this was Egypt, but centuries later, Jesus made clear in his teachings that it was time for them to stop being so literal and to look beyond the physical world to what it symbolises. In John 8:15+ff, he says to the Jewish leaders and teachers,

> 'You decide according to what you can see and touch. I don't make judgements like that. But even if I did, my judgement would be true because I wouldn't make it out of the narrowness of my experience but in the largeness of the One who sent me, the Father,' (*The Message*)

Again we come across this different way of judging things — not simply from personal experience but in the light of God himself. Jesus urges his contemporaries — and by implication, those who seek to follow him — to raise their focus from their own affairs and realise that they are a tiny part of the whole picture. We may not be able to see the whole picture ourselves, 'but we know a man who can', so to speak.

The impression of the Father given by Jesus, both here and in other places, is of one who is larger than we think, who operates on the grand scale, who gives us freedom and space to find our place in the bigger scheme of things, who gives us access to a whole new level of interests and concerns. The suggestion is that if we do not see, even dimly, that his perspective is the true one, we will be trapped by the smallness of our own experiences and viewpoints. The comparison with the development of a child from self-absorption to a wider awareness is relevant here also. A child who is loved and knows it, can make that transition.

6. Task/Question (Group)

Consider the proposition that God himself is the essential dimension without which the things in our experience do not add up and that if we make anything else the touchstone of truth, we may end up in slavery of one kind or another.

*

Section 7

In many of the early chapters of John's gospel, this sense of God the Father being Jesus' focus, is predominant. Jesus performs sign after sign pointing beyond the literal and physical world to the kingdom of God. Again and again his hearers — even the disciples themselves — become obsessed with literal meanings which make nonsense of what Jesus is saying. Nicodemus thinks that being 'born again' is about entering his mother's womb a second time. Jesus' response comes across freshly in Peterson's translation:

> 'You're not listening. Let me say it again. Unless a person submits to this original creation — the 'wind hovering over the water' creation, *the invisible moving the visible*, a baptism into new life — it's not possible to enter God's kingdom. When you look at a baby, it's just that: a body you can look at and touch. But *the person who takes shape within is formed by something you can't see and touch — the Spirit* — and becomes a living spirit.'
> (John 3:5-8, *The Message*: italics mine)

We are so wedded to what we call the empirical or scientific method that we can be blind to the world of the spirit. We need to rethink the relationship between the visible and the invisible. Jesus' point in this and the other signs he performs is that we can't see the wood for the trees. Take the miraculous feeding of the crowd in John 6. Again Peterson's version highlights the point well. Some people saw what was going on —

> 'The people realized that God was at work among them in what Jesus had just done' (v.14)

while others were distracted by the physical manifestation and its implications. —

> 'You've come looking for me not because you saw God in my actions but because I fed you, filled your stomachs — and for free.' (v.26)

and,

> 'Don't waste your energy striving for perishable food... Work for the food that sticks with you, food that nourishes your lasting life, food that the Son of Man provides.' (v.27)

Amongst theologians, hope is known as one of the three theological virtues, the other two being faith and love as outlined in the famous passage in 1 Corinthians 13. The distinction between a theological virtue and either a moral or an intellectual virtue is that the latter two types of virtue, according to Aquinas, a mediaeval theologian, relate to natural affairs, whereas a theological virtue relates to the supernatural realm. This brings us back to the challenge to look beyond the obvious or literal or physical world, though never, of course, to think it unimportant. In fact, once we have a secure grasp of spiritual reality, the physical world can assume for us a wonderful significance as an essential means of expressing the spirit, and this is why John always refers to Jesus' miracles as signs which point to something beyond themselves. The physical world can never be unimportant because it always carries a spiritual message, even though many are deaf to it and most others hear it indistinctly or sporadically.

7. Task/Question (Group)

Find another example in John 6 where Jesus' hearers take him literally and miss his point. Try to express in your own way what their misunderstanding was.

*

Section 8

Building our hope on the character of God, therefore, means making an effort to find out what his main concerns are; not because he needs our support or understanding, but because it is only when we begin to line up with his purposes, that we are set free from baser purposes which will sooner or later enslave us.

This change of perspective involves seeing the physical world around us — wonderful though it is — not as an end in itself, but as a symbol of a deeper reality. Some of the worst excesses of mistaken Christian zeal in history have arisen from a failure to see this. Think of the efforts of the Crusaders to capture the literal city of Jerusalem or any of the more grotesque machinations surrounding the physical land of Israel throughout modern history. We do untold damage when we confuse the literal with the symbolic. False hopes can be pinned on worldly and physical goals and can only end in disillusionment and bitterness. Jesus eluded the effort to make him king because he knew it was based on this blinkered view of reality. His kingdom was not a worldly one, he always maintained.

This same error crops up amongst atheists and agnostics. It often takes the form of thinking that the only happiness we can hope for consists in the good things this life has to offer: good health or wealth or a happy family life or even success, fame, achievement — any number of good things and the belief that if we do not have these, we have no importance or significance. To one who holds such a view, death is the end of all hope. The best that can be expected is to be remembered fondly by loved ones, or to have left many children or good works as a legacy to posterity.

It's true that these are important matters. Unbreakable hope, however, is a much less fragile thing altogether. It relates to what the Bible calls 'the kingdom of heaven' and is not dependent on happiness or success as we normally think of them. Exploring this more certain kind of hope will constitute the main body of this study; but I would remind anyone who fears it will be 'too heavenly to be any earthly use', that Jesus urged us to pray that God's will should be done on earth as it is in heaven, and that the kingdom of heaven has a great impact on the ordinary things of life. We need to ask what we can honestly hope for in this life and still be true to its deeper meaning.

8. Task/Question (Group)
Read Matthew 24:6-14 (*NIV*) and consider what impact these verses might have on our hope for this world.

*

Section 9

On the face of it, these prophecies in Matthew's gospel may seem rather grim, but there are some real positives in amongst them, such as: 'see to it that you are not alarmed', or 'these are the beginning of birth-pains', or 'he who stands firm to the end will be saved' or 'this gospel of the kingdom will be preached in the whole world'. To pick out even one of them — 'these are the beginning of birth-pains' —

gives an essential sense of purpose to the hardships outlined here. 'What is being so painfully born?' we may legitimately ask. What could be so wonderful that it would be worth struggling through all that for? Why not cut to the chase and leave out all the labour? There must be something very necessary in the process if our God, in whom there is no darkness at all, declares that 'such things must happen'. And who even more strangely, can also say, having warned that wars will occur, 'Blessed are the peacemakers, for they will be called sons of God' (Matthew 5:9 *NIV*)

If we think back to the idea of parents having hopes for their children, and consider what God as father may hope for his children, perhaps we will gain some insight into these mysteries. No earthly parents want to see their own beloved children facing hardships, and yet there comes a point at which they feel it is appropriate for the loved child to be exposed to difficult realities so that he or she can find out how to handle them and be stretched and challenged to find creative responses. This is a frighteningly risky stage, as the developing character can respond in damaging ways or fall into all sorts of traps. Yet without some risk, maturity cannot come about, so the parents have to put some trust in the child they have brought up and let him or her make the inevitable mistakes on the way to adulthood. Good parents can let go in that way and yet be ready to offer support in the process when needed.

This may suggest some of the personal benefits of hard times, but there is of course the further huge issue thrown up by this passage of how we can have real hope in a world in which such terrible things not only happen, but have been described as necessary in some way. Where is the God in whom there is no darkness at all when darkness seems to be prevailing?

We are in good company when we ask this question, as many of the psalmists called out in distress to God and of course Jesus himself called out from the cross, 'My God, my God, why have you forsaken me?' a cry from the heart as well as a quotation from Psalm 22. He felt the need to ask this terrible question, even though he had told the disciples beforehand that his suffering was a necessary part of his work. Obviously unbreakable hope must be supernaturally robust if it is to sustain us in the face of such shattering events. Both the natural world and the activities of humanity are in a state of massive dislocation so much of the time. Why?

9. Task/Question (Group)

What truth is demonstrated by the wickedness and chaos we see around us — sometimes in small, discouraging ways in our day-to-day existence, and sometimes in tragedies of catastrophic proportions?

*

Section 10

Finally, we cannot engage in a study of hope which does not address our hope for the next life, our hope to be with him in paradise, as Jesus promised the dying thief beside him on the cross. This aspect of our topic might also encompass whatever we take the return of Christ to mean, in its impact upon both this world and the next — perhaps even providing an essential link between the two.

One of the most intense human experiences of hope is when we expect and long to see the faces of loved ones from whom we have been separated. To meet again is to enjoy the communion for which we all long. It should come as no surprise therefore that this hope is the reflection of a longing in the very heart of God himself which he expresses in many ways. This should encourage us to share in the hope of God himself which he is not ashamed to reveal openly to us:

> 'I will dwell among the Israelites and be their God.....who brought them out of Egypt so that I might dwell among them.'
> (Exodus 29:45-46 *NIV*) — God's words about his chosen people in the Old Testament, or:

> 'You've no idea how much I have looked forward to eating this Passover meal with you before I enter my time of suffering. It's the last one I'll eat until we all eat it together in the kingdom of God' (Luke 22:15-16 *The Message*) — Jesus' words to his disciples at the last supper, or:

> 'Father, I want those you have given me to be with me where I am, and to see my glory.'
> (John 17:24 *NIV*) — Jesus' prayer for his disciples.

The result of this association between God and his people is always the same — the more we look, the more glorious we become, as 2 Corinthians 3:18 says:

'We, who with unveiled faces all reflect the Lord's glory, are being transformed into his likeness with ever increasing glory.' (*NIV*)

These verses and others like them would suggest that the deepest hope we can have as human beings is the hope of the glory of God. In fact, it can be such a deep hope that we may not even be aware that this is the longing of our hearts. In other places the glory of God is described as 'the beauty of holiness' — or perhaps we could think of it as the sheer splendour of his goodness.

Often the idea of seeing such goodness face to face might inspire fear or a feeling of unworthiness, rather than hope; or we might be so deep in the toils of troubles or preoccupations, that the heavenly vision seems unreal or far away. I believe it is the particular concern of the Lord to call to us in the middle of our guilt, suffering or busyness and to set our feet on the pilgrim's path of hope, to lead us through the darkness and into his glorious light. As we deal with the difficulties of our various journeys, may our capacity for that glorious reunion be created and deepened.

10. Task/Question (Group)
Read John 14:2+3. How do you interpret this saying of Jesus?

Chapter 2: Setting our Sights

Section 1

A Hope-filled Community Project.

About four months ago, I was given a letter at church on Sunday morning about a prayer project entitled, '40 Days for £40,000'. It had been sent round local churches — as well as many national churches and even further afield — informing us of a commitment made by the trustees and associates of an organisation called 'The Caladh Trust'. 'Caladh' is a Gaelic word meaning 'haven' and it had been adopted as the name of a project designed to help addicts, their families and carers. After several years of such work initiated by a local minister and his mentor who had been involved in similar work elsewhere, a building — 'An Caladh' — had been acquired as a centre for the work, and the organisers had committed themselves to intensive prayer over 40 days, for the work, the people and the finances required to take the project on to its next stage. These organisers were seeking the help of the wider church — in terms of prayer and money — to realise the dream.

40 days, of course, is the time used in the Bible to indicate a time of waiting or testing, prior to an outpouring of blessing or fulfilment. I'm sure I was one of many receiving the leaflet to be moved by the commitment of this group of people on behalf of the needy in our own community, and my spirit went out to them and to the compassionate work they had undertaken as a response to that need.

I heard very shortly afterwards, that they had more than met their target, having had the exciting experience of seeing approximately £1,000 per day coming in over the 40 days they had set aside for the purpose, and more later. However, as is often the case, the focus of their prayers changed during the 40 days, as that was the time of the terrible storm in our islands and the awful loss of life in one local family, a loss that affected the whole community. The praying group found themselves praying for this situation more than for the Caladh funding, as it was a time for solidarity in grief, as we faced our own mini-tsunami.

More recently, I sought out Iain MacAskill, the minister who initiated the work of Caladh, in order to find out more about the project and to explore how it illustrates aspects of the unbreakable hope we are studying. I also met Penny MacKinnon Macleod, who had been employed part-time as a counsellor and to advise on the future direction of the project. One of her main concerns was that people emerging from addiction should be able to enter a fuller quality of life altogether, not simply to be free of dependency. She believes that the new building will facilitate such progress.

Iain's approach to the whole project seemed to me to be a great example of the perseverance mentioned in the progression from suffering to hope outlined in the passage in Romans 5, which we looked at in the previous chapter. Something like eight years ago, having identified the addiction problem in our community as he went about his pastoral duties, he saw the building which Caladh now own and had the vision of it as a place where God's work to bring healing of this ill might take place. Refusing to be discouraged by unsuccessful attempts to obtain it, he and the team of people who began to share that vision, continued with the detailed business of bringing it to fruition. Some of the 'spin-offs' have all the hallmarks of God's dealings with those who love him and with the communities in which they live.

Because the property was larger than they needed, negotiations were entered into with three other community groups looking for premises and a joint purchase was made ensuring that the Caladh project would be thoroughly integrated into the community, a benefit if the clients are to feel it is for them. Some of the organisations with which the trustees had dealings, it turned out, needed help in coping with some of their own employees caught up in addiction, and the very formation of the trust itself involved fruitful contact between different denominations and churches as well as liaisons with government and local agencies who contributed substantially to both funding and services offered. A work that began under the auspices of the kirk session of a local congregation is now continuing as an independent Christian charitable trust, which employs three part-time workers and attracts many volunteers.

Although the work had a Christian inspiration, those running it are clear that what they are offering is for anyone who needs it without conditions. It is a caring service, not an attempt to convert. Another interesting spin-off is the provision of donated and restored furniture for families who are in need or have been homeless. The building also looks promising as a gathering point for people suffering from rural isolation.

Iain says that moments of uncertainty occurred as all the organisers had to become clear that the large sums of money required for the property were truly warranted, and other issues had to be resolved, for example, when some cooperating community groups proposed fundraising efforts involving large quantities of alcohol. He hopes that attitudes to excessive drinking in our society will change, just as they have to smoking in recent years.

I saw the property in its final stages of refurbishment. It has all the signs of a building well adapted to its proposed use, having comfortable spaces and being well integrated into other community facilities. I also met David Kirk, another of the part-time employees, responsible for the administrative side of the project — an enthusiast who had thought of the 40 days idea.

Looking at the work as a whole, it seems to me that it is a wonderful illustration of the way that the kingdom of heaven can have a profound effect upon a community. Individuals and then whole groups of people are inspired to reach out in some way towards those who are trapped in the toils of a destructive way of life. This is the desire to set the prisoners free about which Jesus spoke to his generation. In the process of reaching out, they are given the chance to experience greater freedom themselves and the excitement of being involved in something which God himself is orchestrating, and which, therefore, has all sorts of unexpected and beneficial ramifications. This team and the project itself have found favour in the whole local community.

1. Task/Question (Group)

Can you think of an enterprise you know of, which has this same mark of God's hand upon it? If not, itemise the signs of grace shown by the example above.

*

Section 2

When I consider this project, the one issue which stands out to me particularly is the way that addiction of any kind makes a prisoner of a person. The Caladh project workers seek to facilitate the bringing of release to addicts, but they themselves are aware of their own 'addictions' which may have less dramatic effects than those of their clients, but still restrict and obstruct their ability to live life to the full. This is something we are all aware of to a greater or lesser degree in our own experience, and there is a connection between this and unbreakable hope, which may be worth exploring.

So much of our experience seems to be characterised by struggle with ourselves over issues such as diet, exercise, smoking, overspending or meanness, overworking or laziness, inappropriate sexual desire, inordinate desire to make money, excessive acquisitiveness — obsessions of one kind or another which seem to dominate our lives. Even a seemingly innocent hobby can assume inordinate importance, making us slaves to sports fixtures and the like. Why is this the case? What are we expecting from the object of our obsession? Relief from emptiness or pain or fear?

Responses vary. Some indulge their every whim and go after instant gratification and messy, damaging lives result. Others impose a rigid control on themselves which can itself misfire in the shape of disorders such as anorexia nervosa — or worse — a sort of bitter, kill-joy attitude to life. I suppose many of us alternate between self-indulgence and over-rigid control in a generally unsatisfactory way. Why are we stuck in this sort of tension for much of the time, our lives lurching from one extreme to another or proceeding in an erratic, unconstructive way? What can lift us out of this stop-start situation?

The Biblical answer is a change of focus — to take attention away from the things we obsess about, and put it on God and his concerns.

2. Task/Question (Group)

Read Matthew 6:19-34. It is particularly fresh and lively in *The Message* translation; e.g. verses 25-26: 'If you decide for God, living a life of God-worship, it follows that you don't fuss about what's on the table at mealtimes or whether the clothes in your closet are in fashion. There is far more to your life than the food you put in your stomach, more to your outer appearance than the clothes you hang on your body. Look at the birds, free and unfettered, not tied down to a job description, careless in the care of God. And you count far more to him than birds.' And verse 33: 'Steep your life in God-reality, God-initiative, God-provisions. Don't worry about missing out. You'll find all your everyday human concerns will be met.'

*

Section 3

Finding out, and focussing on, God's concerns is a sound strategy, but there are at least two aspects of this that may need further consideration: firstly, paying attention to what God is doing needs practice; it is a skill that needs to be learned. I will return to this later, but first let us consider the second aspect — that is, that our obsessions or addictions may have too firm a grip for us to be able to lay them down at will. We may need to be specifically set free from them. Our ability to lay them aside may have been compromised by long association with them.

In a specific, physical addiction, such as alcoholism, this is manifested in the body's dependence on alcohol, and acute withdrawal symptoms on deprivation of it; but any other 'addiction', whether physical, emotional, social, intellectual or even spiritual, can have as strong a hold over us, even though it may not be seen so clearly at first. After all, these obsessions are often entered into as some sort of self-preservation mechanism, and unless the underlying issues have been tackled, the defence mechanism may be held onto with a deceptively loose grasp.

The classic attitude of the sufferer is that he or she could leave the obsession at any time, so deceiving the self as well as other people. What I am saying is that, for example, it may be easier for a person — say — to struggle with constant dieting and bingeing, than to accept that the dissatisfaction with self that he or she is feeling, may need to be tackled at a deeper level. The illusion that, given just a little more time, I could sort myself out, is a seductive one. It takes bravery and clear-sightedness and often support from other people, to admit defeat over an issue and seek help, perhaps to ask for prayer, to give up trying to fix oneself and to throw oneself on God's mercy, waiting for his saving action to bring about change at a deep level.

3. Task/Question (By yourself)
Consider whether there is an issue like this in your own life, and if so, whether you are ready to ask to be set free from it. Be prepared to ask a trusted friend or spiritual advisor to help you.

*

Section 4

Before we arrive at such a state of addiction, we may be able to nip the growing obsession in the bud. It can, after all be a good tendency that has simply gone awry.

It seems to be part of the human condition to be forever hoping for something more or better than what we are or have. In fact such an attitude could have its benefits because in the right spirit it could prompt us to grow and develop until we reach our full potential. However, it is very easy to hitch this basic motivation to unworthy objects and in the heat of the chase to forget more important matters.

We only have to consider any pastime for which we do not have a natural affinity to see how inexplicable is the time, effort, energy and money other people are prepared to expend in pursuing an end that hardly seems worth the trouble. This is not, of course, to condemn the natural and healthy enjoyment and benefit of any innocent pastime which does no harm to others or the environment. Rather, it is to appeal for a sense of the relative importance of the activity in the context of life as a whole. Again, this is not to despise the recreational and essential revitalising aspects of any leisure time activity, nor to deny that lessons learned in play can usefully be transferred to more serious aspects of our lives. What can happen, however, is that an activity such as this can become a way of avoiding issues that need to be addressed, or a false way of giving meaning to an empty life.

Such displacement, however, can attach itself to more serious contenders: for example, my job can become the 'be all and end all'; my romantic relationships can clamour for centre stage; even church work of a generally valuable kind can become obsessive. We can become over-intense about 'good' as well as 'bad' aspects of our lives.

4. Task/Question (By yourself)

Try to identify something in your own experience which has assumed an inordinate importance for you, when considered in the context of your life as a whole. Ask yourself why this has happened.

*

Section 5

I should like to return to the issue of learning to focus on God's interests rather than our own — especially the point that it is a skill that can be acquired. This may be particularly necessary immediately after a release from some sort of addiction or obsession — and in fact may be an essential element in that release. As is the case with the learning of any new skill, practice makes perfect.

If you decide to learn to play a musical instrument, you will set aside — say — half an hour a day to play scales, do exercises and learn pieces. You will go, perhaps weekly, to an expert, for instruction, and very gradually, things which seemed impossible for you, will begin to happen. The co-ordination, manual dexterity, rhythm and accurate tuning will begin to feature in your playing, though it may sound terrible at first, and perhaps for some time. Some aspects of the skill may seem more difficult to acquire than others and may need more work. You will find some pieces more congenial than others, and you will discover that you have a flair for certain aspects of the process.

There will be times of discouragement when you doubt that you will ever master the instrument, and other times of breakthrough when success will drive you to take longer at your practice than usual.

Eventually, your growing competence will make practice more of a pleasure and you will be ready to spend more time on it and to tackle more advanced pieces. You will also be able to sight-read simpler pieces without having learned them. When you are at an advanced stage of the process, you may even consider taking pupils of your own and/or performing in a concert for the entertainment of others. If this sounds too much like hard work to anyone, he or she probably did not really have a deep enough desire to master the skill in the first place. Usually what motivates a person to learn to play an instrument, is hearing someone else play well and being inspired to emulate.

So, what are the 'scales and exercises' a person needs to practise if he is to learn to focus on God's concerns? Some of the essentials are surely to consider how God has dealt with people, what he has done, what he has said, how he has presented himself and how he responds to people and events. This can take many forms, for example: talking and listening to people whose experience of God rings true; reading about them in the Bible or in other books; taking the time to listen to our own spirits as they are instructed by the Holy Spirit in prayer; seeing what can be understood of God from studying his creation; trying to do what he wants as far as we know it, for example, reaching out to needy people or forgiving those who have wronged us; gathering with others to worship God and perhaps most importantly, looking at his self-portrait in the person of Jesus Christ.

5. Task/Question (By yourself)

Read Philippians 4:6-9. Take fifteen minutes to think about 'things true, noble, reputable … etc.' from your experience. Discipline yourself not to digress into complaints, disappointments etc. for the full fifteen minutes.

*

Section 6

We may well ask what the connection is between unbreakable hope and learning the skill of focussing on God's concerns. The answer must surely be to do with the importance of knowing what we can legitimately hope for. It is so easy to underestimate how 'noisy' our own urgent concerns are. They make so much noise in our consciousness that the 'still, small voice' of God, drawing attention to our true and most important concerns, is drowned out. With regard to spiritual truth, we are like someone listening to a distant voice on a telephone with a faulty line while all our children are playing noisily in the same room and the T.V. is blaring. In order to hear the voice, we have to switch off the T.V. and put the children to bed. We have to refuse the clamouring of the 'urgent' in order to pay attention to the 'important'.

This is by no means an easy task. It is so much easier to stay on the familiar treadmill of our usual, hectic, obsessive or anxious thinking or activity, than to face the unknown and maybe scary stillness of the unpredictable voice of God. 'Be still and know that I am God' as the psalmist puts it. Ironically, it is the 'still, small voice' that brings the key that will eventually put all the issues we think of as so urgent into a proper perspective, but we can only arrive at this perspective by quieting our own efforts and trusting the inner voice.

In order to be able to entrust ourselves to this voice, we have to have at least a dim picture of God as infinitely good. This is why Jesus began his ministry by quoting Isaiah:

> "God's Spirit is on me; he's chosen me to preach the Message of good news to the poor, sent me to announce pardon to prisoners and recovery of sight to the blind, to set the burdened and battered free, to announce, 'This is God's year to act."
> (Luke 4:18-19, *The Message*)

Then Jesus followed it up by saying:

> 'You've just heard Scripture make history. It came true just now in this place.' (Luke 4:21, *The Message*)

He knew that compassionate words followed up by compassionate actions in healing and restoring people were the starting point if anyone was to put his or her trust in him. We need to build up our picture of God in this way, so that we base our hope upon his character.

6. Task/Question (Group)

Read 1 John 4:16b "God is love, whoever lives in love lives in God, and God in him." (NIV) To fill out the meaning of this, read 1 Corinthians 13:4-7 (NIV)

*

Section 7

It may have become clear that, as we have been considering the issues that can trip us up in our attempts to hope properly, what needs to change primarily, is not our circumstances or other people — although changes in these may also be necessary — it is our own attitudes and priorities. By the time the difficult circumstance or person has been changed or resolved, the importance of such a change can seem to be almost irrelevant or outdated. Its urgency may have waned as our focus has moved on from it. This is the sign to us that we are growing in perception and in our capacity to distinguish between absolute and relative importance. We are then in a position to make use of the various promises Jesus made to his followers just before his death: for example,

> 'Whatever you request along the lines of who I am and what I'm doing, I'll do it.' (John 14: 13-14, *The Message*) or:

> 'If you make yourselves at home with me and my words are at home in you, you can be sure that whatever you ask will be listened to and acted upon.' (John 15: 7, *The Message*) or:

> 'Ask the Father for whatever is in keeping with the things I've revealed to you.' (John 16: 23, *The Message*)

All of these promises show us how to exercise hope properly — that is in accordance with the character of Christ, and therefore of God himself. At first we may find it difficult to see this as anything other than a restriction, but in fact it is an amazing opening up of divine power to ordinary people. Before the first of these promises, Jesus shows the astonishing and risky generosity of his offer, in these words:

> 'The person who trusts me will not only do what I'm doing but even greater things, because I, on my way to the Father, am giving you the same work to do that I've been doing. You can count on it.'

There is an aspect of this work that is the same as Jesus' own work — it is of the same spirit — but there is an aspect that is greater than his work, because it can be done by all who trust him. Each of these people will have different gifts and will ask for different blessings, each of which will show a distinctive aspect of God's character.

More than that, the particular flavour of each trusting person's answered prayers will be unique. This exercise of divine power is a genuine sharing in the creative work of God himself and gives him the sort of delight that a teacher may experience when he learns something from his or her pupil, or that a parent may experience when his child brings a distinctive contribution to the solution of a family problem. As Jesus said on the same occasion:

> I've told you these things for a purpose: that my joy might be your joy, and your joy wholly mature' (John 15: 11, *The Message*)

The practice of creative love is always a joyful one though not without cost.

7. Task/Question (By yourself)

Dig deep into your own spirit to find a Christ-like desire there. Nurture it until you can see how to pray for the first step in its fulfilment. Note down what you prayed and then look out for the answer. Keep as open a mind as possible about how the answer will come.

*

Section 8

By now in this study, you should have formed the impression that learning how to hope properly could be a lifetime's occupation, and in many ways this is true. By the time we reach the end of our lives, this discipline will have trained us to long for the closer presence of Christ that he promised his followers. However, lest this seems too far away, out of reach or impossible, we need to remember that our hope's fulfilment is not a reward for services rendered. Nor is it a state of enlightenment achieved by rigorous self denial or ascetic practices. It is not something we could ever earn or deserve. God does not owe us a thing. In fact he takes delight in giving unexpected gifts and insights to unlikely and undeserving candidates, which demonstrates his total freedom and generosity and undercuts any build up of unwarranted human pride.

The parable of the workers who were hired at different times of day (Matthew 20) shows an employer who pays a decent day's wages for a decent day's work but who also chooses to give the full wage to those who have only worked for part of the day. This illustrates God's delight in blessing the undeserving and shows how anyone who trusts his generosity may have free access to his goodness while knowing himself unworthy of it. This is the same as the point about not trying to fix ourselves before coming to God. Rather, we should come to him without delay and trust him to fix us. Jesus has already finished God's work of restoring everything, ourselves included. The only 'work' required of us is to believe it and to benefit from it.

The disciplines we undergo do not make us more deserving, they make us more able to believe in God's good purposes for the undeserving, and therefore more able to benefit from them. In other words, we get to know him better, learn how to receive his love and experience the transformation that a certainty of being loved brings. Because we then have a sense of plenty ourselves, we have no difficulty in being generous to others as the insecurity of competition has disappeared. There is more than enough for all. The striving of obsessive behaviour is shown to be unnecessary. The truth has set us free.

8. Task/Question (Group)

Look again at the parable of the lost son in Luke 15:vv.11+ff. Compare the attitudes of the prodigal and his older brother to the father in the story. (vv.21+29) Then compare the attitude of the father to the two sons. (vv.20+31) Do you think undue favouritism was shown to the younger son?

*

Section 9

As we learn to focus on God's priorities more and more, and the direction of our hope becomes truer, our habits of thought, the 'neural pathways' of our spirits begin to reflect his image more accurately. However, what we experience in our lives — the people we meet, the current events of our country and our world, what we read and hear, so much of what we are exposed to every minute of every day — gives quite a contrary message, which constantly undermines the 'retuning' of ourselves onto God's wavelength. Even those experienced in the ways of God can lose sight of what they know and slide into their old, habitual way of thinking. Almost without realising it, instead of holding out against faulty, facile interpretations of affairs, which leave God out of the equation altogether, they begin to think in ways which lead back into 'prison'.

All the same, someone who has experienced real freedom usually remembers the taste of it and can revisit the springs of refreshment when he begins to sense the constrictions of false thinking. This would be a time to return to some of the 'scales and exercises' outlined above as a way of focussing on God's purposes.

The one I personally find best in such circumstances is talking and listening to those whose experience of God rings true. This can give one the sense of a community of people whose thinking has been rinsed clean by God's word. Such people seem free of obsession; they have a sort of distance between themselves and their desires which inspires confidence in their judgement and in the balanced nature of their views; they are at one's disposal in a way that is distinctive and seems more 'human'. Such a person is truly 'present' and available and a real help in trouble — not always by doing anything in particular, but simply by being there. He or she causes difficulties to recede from overwhelming levels by reminding us of what is true and what is important.

9. Task/Question (By yourself)

Think of a person like this in your acquaintance. Seek out him or her and start drawing out his or her thoughts and wisdom. It doesn't really matter what subject you discuss because that freedom from self will allow life-giving truth to emerge and your perspective will be restored.

*

Section 10

For the last section of this chapter, I would like to reflect on one of the other ways certain Christians have adopted, usually — though not always — for a limited period of time, in order to gain, refresh or maintain this perspective. It is the practice of going into retreat of one kind or another, for example, going off alone into the wild as Jesus himself did just prior to his ministry.

At various times in the history of the church, some believers have found it helpful to go into the desert, or to become hermits, to live on a lonely island or equivalent, to spend time in seclusion within a religious community, even to go alone to a cabin in the woods for a while. A few stay there and take up the contemplative life or adopt a lifestyle of intercessory prayer, sometimes receiving those who seek them out for spiritual counsel, but most find it best as a temporary expedient and as a help towards realigning themselves with God's will/the truth/their true selves.

After being apart for a while, they are then equipped for whatever they are called to be or do in the world, and can return to a greater level of direct involvement in human affairs, but having gained some protection against becoming engrossed in a distorting way. Whatever strategies we adopt to keep a true perspective on life, it is the *purpose* of these strategies that is the important thing. In this connection I would like to quote the beginning of a poem by Paulinus of Nola which expresses something of that purpose. Paulinus, the Bishop of Nola in Italy at the end of the fourth century and beginning of the fifth century, was the foremost Latin poet of the Patristic period of Church History.

Desert Christians

Not that they beggared be in mind, or brutes,
That they have chosen a dwelling place afar
In lonely places: but *their eyes are turned*
To the high stars, the very deep of Truth.
Freedom they seek, an emptiness apart
From worthless hopes: din of the market place
And all the noisy crowding up of things,
And whatever wars on the Divine,
At Christ's command, and for his love, they hate.
By faith and hope they follow after God,
And know their quest shall not be desperate,
If but the present conquer not their souls
With hollow things: that which they see they spurn,
That they may come at what they don't see,
Their senses kindled like a torch that may
Blaze through the secrets of eternity.
(Italics mine.)

10. Task/Question (By yourself)

What environment do you personally find most conducive to this purpose of restoring perspective and focussing on God's priorities? Do you have enough access to this environment? If not, what can you do about it? Bear in mind that this is a profound spiritual need and not a luxury and so would be a very legitimate prayer request.

Chapter 3: What's in a Name?

Section 1

In this chapter I would like to tackle a difficult issue, but one which may need to be faced if we do not wish to lose our grasp on unbreakable hope.

It is the matter of those who purport to be followers of Christ, but whose character, words or behaviour is not conducive to encouragement and hope of a real nature. This is an issue historically. Look at the record of so-called Christian activity in the world with its many shortcomings and even cruelty and oppression in the name of Christ. It can also be an issue if we read or hear church leaders' statements about social or political issues which are reactionary, ignorant, mealy-mouthed or lacking in compassion. It can be an issue if we experience small-mindedness, strife, self-righteousness, indifference, avarice, worldliness or fanaticism in the ranks of 'Christian' churches of our acquaintance. Where are our grounds for hope if those who should be its exponents so often put up such a pitiful show?

First of all, there is the principle that, 'no news is good news', and the fact that countless thousands of Christians are — and always have been — working away self-sacrificially in the background with vision, integrity, compassion, wisdom and love to improve the lot of those with whom they come in contact. We can help to correct the bias of the news (towards disgrace and disaster) by spreading news of any of these we know about. A more accurate picture of the church and its role would undoubtedly emerge, as many Christian congregations throughout our land, and indeed the world, are communities of people of goodwill who genuinely are the 'salt of the earth' and who work tirelessly to 'bring in God's kingdom' in their respective spheres of work and influence, allowing the Spirit of Christ to inform their relationships with their families, neighbours, workmates and with their natural environments also.

They are an army of people who serve, teach, heal, preach, administer, campaign, counsel, judge, defend, keep the peace, promote law and order, bring up children, run efficient and fair businesses, make and give money to worthy causes, raise consciousness about important issues, report on events in dangerous places, offer a challenge to oppressive regimes, write good imaginative literature, carry out research, deal with emergencies, practise sound agricultural procedures, befriend the lonely, provide entertainment of quality, practise good workmanship in a trade, protect the environment, offer sound and fair financial services, preserve our historical heritage, care for the infirm and perform a host of other useful and beneficial tasks, which may or may not hit the headlines. Often it is only the beneficiaries of these tasks and those in their immediate vicinity who know about them.

Of course, these functions can also be performed well, and in many cases, better, by those who have no specific Christian commitment, or who embrace another faith. Likewise, people who are not followers of Christ can generate the harmful effects outlined above, militating against hope in our world. The problem under discussion arises when those who claim to represent the specifically Christian hope we are considering, do not in fact provide good examples of it themselves. In such cases, we may legitimately ask what difference it makes to embrace such a hope, if it does not always mean that the people who do so are changed for the better by it.

It may seem obvious, but what it boils down to, is that, in the realm of human behaviour, nothing is automatic. There is no inevitable connection between what a person receives by way of Christian input or training and the way that person conducts him or herself. Most of us consider that it is good to receive an education, for example. Yet we know that some people make far better use of their education than others. They soak up everything they learn, and in the end, they may outstrip their teachers in original thinking and fruitful applications of their learning. Others go through the school system from beginning to end and seem to benefit very little from it all, or worse, become cleverer criminals. However, we still consider that to be educated is better than to be uneducated, even though we can all point to people whose education has not benefited them or society. Likewise, many of those who call themselves Christian may not act accordingly, yet they may have had every opportunity to absorb and practise the faith they profess. That they were given that opportunity is surely a matter to be celebrated, even though they did not make use of it.

1. Task/Question (Group)
Study two of Jesus' parables about the kingdom of God, the parable of the sower and the parable of the weeds (Matthew 13.1-30+36-43). Can you see any connection between them and this issue?

*

Section 2

If you think the fate of the 'weeds' in the second parable is rather savage, then reflect that they were masquerading as 'wheat', sabotaging the good crop and confusing the onlookers as to the quality of the harvest in the field. Anyone pretending to be good and holy while actually making things harder for poor or weak people, was treated harshly by Jesus. He had no patience or sympathy for religious leaders who simply enjoyed their status as such and who dreamed up oppressive laws for those who were already overburdened, or who felt they were not good enough to approach God. Referring to such leaders, Jesus said to his disciples:

> 'Every tree that wasn't planted by my Father in heaven will be pulled up by its roots. Forget them. They are blind men leading blind men.' (Matthew 15:13-14 *The Message*)

Here, maintaining hope is shown to be a matter of focus. Jesus' advice is not to waste any more time thinking about them, as their fate is sealed already. His concern was to extend the mercy of God to any who were labouring under a false 'yoke' such as these leaders tried to impose upon the vulnerable. The point for our study is that it doesn't matter what people call themselves, it matters what they actually are. In Shakespeare's 'Romeo and Juliet', Juliet laments the fact that Romeo suffers from the prejudice her whole family show towards the Montague family.

> 'What's in a name? That which we call a rose
> By any other name would smell as sweet;
> So Romeo would, were he not Romeo call'd,
> Retain that dear perfection which he owes
> Without that title.' (Act 2, Sc. 2, ll.43-47)

Likewise, anyone who does not call himself a Christian, but regularly acts in the compassionate Spirit of Christ, is in fact 'the real thing'. Conversely, anyone who does call himself a Christian, but regularly belies it by his actions, has been guilty of 'taking the Lord's name in vain' and will be held responsible for doing so. This offence is more about betraying the character of Christ by one's actions than about using God's name as a swear word, though of course that is a part of such betrayal. In the Bible, the name of God is always indissolubly linked with his character and actions, in which — as we are taking as our starting point — there is no darkness at all. In other words, all God's actions express his life-saving love for humankind and the names by which he is known express different aspects of his powerfully effective character, for example, 'El Shaddai' used in Genesis 17:1, which means 'mountain' and symbolises the strength and changelessness so much needed by weak human beings.

2. Task/Question (Group)

Read Jesus' parable about the two sons in Matthew 21: 28-32. Try to analyse what it tells us about appearance and reality in God's service.

*

Section 3

The unguaranteed link between name and character is the key to an understanding and recognition of the Christian church in the world.

'By their fruit you will recognise them' (*NIV*)

as Jesus says in Matthew 7:16. That whole passage in *The Message* warns that those whose behaviour belies the name of Christian will come to no good:

> 'Be wary of false preachers who smile a lot, dripping with practiced sincerity. Chances are they are out to rip you off some way or other. Don't be impressed with charisma; look for character. Who preachers *are* is the main thing, not what they say. A genuine leader will never exploit your emotions or your pocketbook. These diseased trees with their bad apples are going to be chopped down and burned.
>
> Knowing the correct password — saying 'Master, Master,' for instance — isn't going to get you anywhere with me. What is required is serious obedience — *doing* what my Father wills.' (Verses 15-21)

In context, Jesus was referring to the Jewish leaders betraying the name of Yahweh, the great 'I AM' as revealed to the ancient Hebrews. The Old Testament history is the story of this chosen people and their fitful attempts to live up to their calling to bring wholeness to the world. As Yahweh said to Abraham when he first called him:

'All the families of the Earth will be blessed through you.'
(Genesis 12:3. *The Message.*)

The high points of this story include all the great heroes of faith, many of whom are listed in the eleventh chapter of Hebrews along with a summary of their exploits, which are as varied as they themselves are. Yet despite all the wonderful things they did, many of them were no strangers to disgrace either, and the salvation story limps along at times. King David is a good example of someone who embodied all the ideals of kingship, yet he not only had an adulterous relationship with Uriah's wife, Bathsheba, but arranged for Uriah's death in battle when his attempt to pass the child off as Uriah's failed. As Isaiah represents the words of Yahweh in chapter 63 of his prophecy:

> 'I've been treading the winepress alone. No one was there to help me....The time for redemption had arrived. I looked around for someone to help — no one. I couldn't believe it — not one volunteer. So I went ahead and did it myself.'
> (Verses 3a, 4b+5a. *The Message*)

The Christian church has always seen the actions of Jesus as the fulfilment of the promise of wholeness in the Old Testament. His actions are those of God himself, saving not only his chosen people, but also the whole world. In the last analysis, Jesus was the only one who allowed absolutely no separation between his *name*, which means 'God saves', and the *actions* of his whole life and death. The second verse of the hymn, 'At the name of Jesus, every knee shall bow' by Caroline Maria Noel reads:

> 'Humbled for a season,
> To receive a name
> From the lips of sinners
> Unto whom he came,
> Faithfully he bore it
> Spotless to the last;
> Brought it back victorious
> When from death he passed.'

This verse states how the name of 'Saviour' was not given to Jesus in vain. He lived up to his name faithfully in his life by reaching out powerfully and compassionately to everyone who came to him. Then after his death, which he told his followers was for the forgiveness of sin, he returned to life, demonstrating to them that they had no need to fear either death or judgement if they put their faith in him. This 'salvation' brought about by Jesus, has always been at the heart of the Christian message.

The essential quality of Jesus is that there is no disappointment with him. The better he is known, the truer he seems. Attempts to show that he had feet of clay — as even the best of the rest of the heroes of faith have on closer acquaintance — have never been convincing. Even people who dislike or repudiate Christianity in any of its forms, seldom have a problem with the character of Jesus himself. This is why his saving actions are reckoned to be so effective, because like God himself there is no darkness at all in Jesus; on the contrary, his light is such that he is recognised by millions of people as divine as well as human. The writer of Hebrews makes the point we need to hear in this connection. He refers to the original God-given calling of men and women before they went astray:

> 'When God put them in charge of everything, nothing was excluded. But we don't see it yet, don't see everything under human jurisdiction. *What we do see is Jesus.*' (Hebrews 2:8-9 *The Message*, italics mine.)

and:

> 'Keep your eyes on *Jesus*, who both began and finished this race we're in.' (Hebrews 12:2 *The Message*)

Again, maintaining unbreakable hope turns out to be a matter of focus. On what or on whom are we concentrating?

3. Task/Question (By yourself/Group)
Identify an activity you are engaged in — a sport, one of the arts, running a business, whatever — in which success depends almost entirely on keeping your focus right. Try to explain how this works.

*

Section 4

We have been considering the idea that the hope of generations of people of God came to a head in the life and death of Christ. Those who accept this interpretation see Christ's life and death, and more particularly his resurrection, as the major turning point in restoration history, which then turned outwards to the rest of humankind, the imperative of the young Christian church being to spread its message throughout the world.

The way in which this mission is carried out can easily give the lie to the content of the message. This can result in 'Christian' churches spreading something radically different from Christ's original message and the distortion can cause untold damage. In history, there are the notorious attempts to convert by missionaries who carried the cross in one hand and a sword in the other and more recently, there are occasions when receiving various benefits has been made conditional on converting to Christianity. Again, in the realm of human behaviour, nothing is automatically right. If it is possible for someone to preach the gospel from wrong motives or in a way that is at variance with its true spirit, we can be sure it has been done by someone somewhere in the history of the church.

At this point, it may be useful to look again at the terms of the Christian commission, to see what was actually required.

First, at the end of Matthew's gospel, Jesus' instructions to his disciples were:

> 'Go out and *train* everyone you meet, far and near, in this way of life, marking them by baptism in the threefold name: Father, Son, and Holy Spirit. Then instruct them in the *practice* of all I have commanded you.
> (Matthew 28:19-20 *The Message* — italics mine.)

Then, at the end of Luke's gospel, his words are:

> 'You can see how it is written that the Messiah suffers, rises from the dead on the third day, and then *a total life-change* through the forgiveness of sins is proclaimed in his name to all nations — starting from here, from Jerusalem! You're the first to see and hear it. You're the witnesses. What comes next is very important: I am sending what my Father promised to you, so stay here in the city until he arrives, until you're equipped with power from on high.' (Luke 24:46-49 *The Message* — italics mine.)

When Peter preached to the crowd that gathered on the day when the promised 'power from on high' had been given, these were among the words he used:

> *'Change your life.* Turn to God and be baptised, each of you, in the name of Jesus Christ, so your sins are forgiven. Receive the gift of the Holy Spirit. The promise is targeted to you and your children, but also to those who are far away — whomever, in fact, our Master God invites.' (Acts 2:38-39 *The Message* — italics mine.)

I have chosen these extracts and italicised certain words in order to emphasise the fact that the great commission is not simply a question of persuading people to sign on the dotted line or to become a member of a club. It is not just a matter of calling yourself a Christian or associating with other Christians out of accident, habit or custom. It is not even necessarily something that can be done in a moment of time and then you're 'in' and you can be forgotten about. It is rather a way of life.

When people embark on this way of life, their lives may be chaotic, damaged, in disarray — even harmful to themselves and others. In some cases, there is a decisive moment of encounter with Christ in which sudden change occurs followed by a daily learning of the new and more wholesome ways he generates. In other cases, there is a gradual realisation of Christ's centrality and a continuing absorption of these ways. At any point in these processes, a person can become stuck, distracted, discouraged or put off by hardships which crop up. Nothing is automatic. There is no guarantee that the new convert will progress to maturity without a hitch. Christians are not made by magic or against their will. The Spirit of God begins the deep and detailed process of bringing a person to wholeness with the cooperation of that person. It is like bringing up a child. Of course there is happiness and delight at the birth of the child, but the deeper joy comes when the child grows, matures and realises the potential of infancy.

4. Task/Question (Group)
What do you think of the idea of resolving not to have children at all because the whole process is so fraught with danger and because the world we live in can be so damaging to vulnerable human beings? Is there a valid parallel with the process of making people

disciples of Christ? Should we resolve not to encourage conversion because there are so many ways in which the development of the new Christian can miscarry?

Section 5

In the light of all this, it must be clear that the groups of people who call themselves the Christian church will be a complete mixture of fake and true, mature and immature. Unbreakable hope cannot depend on the integrity of everyone who calls himself or herself a Christian. We cannot avoid the difficult process of discerning where the truth lies. Names will not be enough.

In addition to the process of discerning whether an individual is being true to the Spirit of Christ, we have the thorny issue of whether the institution of the church as a structure is conducive to the operation of his Spirit. If the organisation is made up of imperfect people, some at least of its institutional arrangements will be imperfect also, allowing some of the false or immature members into positions of power and influence, where they may try to control the spiritual lives — and even the so-called secular lives — of the other members. This is perhaps one of the greatest stumbling blocks to hope both in the present day and in the history of the Christian church.

At the time of the Reformation, for example, the abuses of power in the institution of the church had become intolerable to those who became reformers. Many of them began with no idea of leaving the church, but wanted to change it from within. In many cases they were either excommunicated or had to leave as they were unable to effect the changes they thought necessary. As the Protestant churches took shape, some of the reformers tried to enshrine the idea of change within their institutions by describing themselves as 'always reforming' rather than 'reformed' churches. They recognised that setting up an institution at all carries the danger of the arrangements solidifying into rigid laws which strangle the essential life of the church and because of that, they emphasised the need for any institution to remain flexible.

Again and again, the various churches have split over a multitude of different issues, ranging from the frankly ridiculous to essential questions which touch on the substance of the faith. Most of the churches newly formed after a split, had grasped an important truth which had become very damagingly neglected by the churches they had left. A host of different modes of church organisation and government have arisen over the years: attempts to allow the essential expression of the body of Christ to be unhindered. What are we to make of this chequered history of the institution of the church as we try to lay hold of the unbreakable hope at its heart?

The gospel of Matthew again has some useful wisdom here, on the subject of authority. Anyone who has suffered under oppressive church authority will find these words of Jesus very liberating:

> 'You all have a single Teacher and you are all classmates. Don't set people up as experts over your life, letting them tell you what to do. Save that authority for God; let him tell you what to do. No one else should carry the title of 'Father'; you have only one Father, and he's in heaven. And don't let people manoeuvre you into taking charge of them. There is only one Life-Leader for you and them — Christ. (Matthew 23:8-10 *The Message*)

Jesus then goes on to describe and exemplify his own style of leadership, which is that of being a servant to those he is leading. It follows that oppressive leadership is not that of Christ himself and therefore is unchristian.

Jesus' own words about the church are worth examining. He makes his key remarks about it when Peter has made his famous declaration, recognising Jesus as, 'The Christ, the Son of the living God':

> 'Jesus came back, 'God bless you, Simon, son of Jonah! You didn't get that answer out of books or from teachers. My Father in heaven, God himself, let you in on this secret of who I really am. And now I'm going to tell you who you are, *really* are. You are Peter, a rock. This is the rock on which I will put together my church, a church so expansive with energy that not even the gates of hell will be able to keep it out. And that's not all. You will have complete and free access to God's kingdom, keys to open any and every door; no more barriers between heaven and earth, earth and heaven. A yes on earth is yes in heaven. A no on earth is no in heaven.' (Matthew 16:17-19 *The Message*)

5. Task/Question (Group)

Some have interpreted this passage to mean that whatever Peter and his successors as church leaders said, should be completely binding upon the church members. Do you agree?

*

Section 6

A useful — if corny — saying is: 'If you find the perfect church, do not join it whatever you do, as it will no longer be perfect.' This contains a very important point, which Christians may or may not be aware of, which is the gap between the name they bear and what they actually are. Anyone who bears the name of Christian with any degree of integrity will sooner or later become conscious of how unlike Christ he or she is.

A review of the passage quoted above will yield good dividends in this connection also. Jesus used two different names for Peter. The first is his birth name, Simon, and this represents how he was in his unchanged self. The second is the name given to him by Christ, Peter, a rock, and this represents what he was to become as he continued to be a follower of Christ. Before the end of the chapter quoted, Christ had to rebuke Peter for trying to persuade Jesus that the suffering he foresaw for himself would not be necessary. Peter's mistakes and failures are clearly recounted in the gospels, yet he was the one whom Jesus chose to be the leader of the young church which Christ said he himself would 'put together'.

Looked at in this light, the imperfections of the church can be a cause for — rather than a barrier to — unbreakable hope, as the church is not a collection of perfect people that 'ordinary folk' cannot be part of. By the same token, if we look at some of the amazing words and actions of Peter in the young church, we can be hopeful that if such a flawed person as Peter can do wonderful things in the name of Christ, perhaps equally wonderful things can be accomplished by 'ordinary' Christians today. This paradox is central to any understanding of the church.

On the one hand, there is the essential forgiveness of God made available to all who know their desperate need of it, illustrated by people such as Peter who knew the bitter grief of having denied Jesus by his words and actions, despite having been determined to follow him to the death. Once Peter's self-knowledge was more accurate, he could be given the chance to reaffirm the Master he had denied and he could be given the responsibilities of church leadership. The chance to begin again on the basis of what Christ has done is an essential aspect of the church's mission. In this respect the door of the church should always be open and none be regarded as a hopeless case. Needy people can be expected to crowd into any place where this right emphasis is made, just as they crowded Jesus during his time on earth and just as three thousand embraced the

Christian way on the day when God empowered the disciples and Peter preached his first sermon.

On the other hand, the crowds around Jesus melted away when following him looked like a dangerous option, and later in the story of the young church, when the awesome acts of the apostles were seen by the crowds, we read:

> 'But even though people admired them a lot, outsiders were wary about joining them.'(Acts 5:13 *The Message)*

There was that about the church which made outsiders uncomfortable. There was an unknown quality amongst them all, something which could not be categorised or controlled, something contrary to their usual way of thinking.

6. Task/Question (By yourself)

Consider your own relationship — or lack of it — with the Christian church. Have you had experience of a branch of it where the leadership was not oppressive, where the forgiveness of God in Christ was emphasised but where you experienced enough challenge to avoid complacency? Spend some time reflecting on this or on imagining it if you have not had such an experience.

*

Section 7

What seems to be emerging from our study is a picture of a flawed organisation which nevertheless has been remarkably resilient overall and in the long-term. Although certain manifestations of the church have disappeared without trace, the organisation as a whole keeps re-inventing itself again and again, as individuals or groups of people either uphold a tradition that is working adequately or break away from traditional modes — or indeed more modern modes — which have become unbearably constricting. Even those who have 'given up' on the visible church altogether bear witness to its importance by the very wounds they carry in their memories of it, which fall so far short of the nourishing place they feel it could or should be.

As Christ left the whole responsibility for the spread of his message in the hands of flawed human beings, this kind of story is perhaps inevitable. At the same time, he promised to be with them in the form of the Holy Spirit, the promised 'power from on high' in one of the passages quoted above. It is worth looking again at some of these words which Peter used on the occasion when the Spirit of God was given to the church:

> 'Receive the gift of the Holy Spirit. The promise is targeted to you and your children, but also to all who are far away — whomever, in fact, our Master God invites.' (Acts 2:38b-39 *The Message*)

and earlier in his sermon:

> 'In the Last Days,' God says, 'I will pour out my Spirit on every kind of people........on those who serve me, men and women both.' (Acts 2:17a+18a *The Message*)

One of the revolutionary aspects of this promise was that the Spirit of God was not only given to special people, as had been the case in the history of the Jewish people, when only those such as prophets, priests or kings were filled with God's Spirit. Here the offer is to everyone who is called by God and although there were to be leaders in the young church, they did not have a monopoly on the Spirit of God. Every believer was to receive the promised Spirit and to exercise the gifts he or she had been given for the benefit of the whole group.

This is a particularly hopeful aspect of the new arrangements for the church, as any member might and would receive essential insights and abilities relating to one or other aspect of the church's life and outreach depending on the gifts he or she had received. It would be the responsibility of the maturer members to nurture the budding gifts of the less mature members and to train them in the proper use of these gifts, so that the body of Christ could work in harmony to build itself up and to reach out into the surrounding community as individuals and sometimes as a group. It must be obvious that an oppressive leadership in such a context could easily suppress the Spirit who seeks full expression through all of the members of the body.

7. Task/Question (By yourself)

Consider again your own relationship — or lack of it — with the Christian church in the light of this point about the Holy Spirit being promised to every member. Is there a branch of the church known to you where every member is encouraged to make an appropriate contribution to the life and outreach of the church?

Section 8

Even this model of the church as the body of Christ with all its members being different parts — outlined by the apostle Paul in 1 Corinthians 12 — has its problems and limitations if the different members start being competitive or are intimidated by one another. This was clearly the case from the beginning as Paul goes straight on from that passage to emphasise the supremacy of love in the famous passage in 1 Corinthians 13, where he makes the point that any gifts exercised without love are worse than useless. Then he outlines the characteristics of Christian love, and this is such a key passage with regard to church life that it is worth quoting again here:

> 'Love never gives up. Love cares more for others than for self. Love doesn't want what it doesn't have. Love doesn't strut, doesn't have a swelled head, doesn't force itself on others, isn't always 'me first', doesn't fly off the handle, doesn't keep score of the sins of others, doesn't revel when others grovel, takes pleasure in the flowering of truth, puts up with anything, trusts God always, always looks for the best, never looks back, but keeps going to the end.' (1 Corinthians 13:4-7 *The Message*)

Perhaps one of the most significant aspects of love considered in the first and last points here is its perseverance. There would be no need to emphasise perseverance if there were not serious threats to love, both in the church and in the world as a whole. Matthew's gospel is again helpful in this regard. Jesus is warning his disciples about the chaos that was to come. He says:

> In the confusion, lying preachers will come forward and deceive a lot of people. For many others, the overwhelming spread of evil will do them in — nothing left of their love but a mound of ashes. *Staying with it — that's what God requires. Stay with it to the end.* You won't be sorry and you'll be saved. All during this time, the good news — the Message of the kingdom — will be preached all over the world, a witness staked out in every country. And then the end will come.' (Matthew 24:11-14 *The Message* italics mine.)

The motivation to 'stay with it' introduces us to another key element of the Christian hope — the promised return of Christ.

Many of the stories Jesus told about the kingdom of God included this question of what he would find us all doing on his return. Will we have 'stayed with it', and expressed this aspect of Christian love? I would like to consider the question of Jesus' return later, but here we are reflecting on the characteristics of the church and whether they constitute a barrier to unbreakable hope or an encouragement to embrace it. In John's gospel Jesus gave a key to recognising the church which focuses very clearly on the question of love:

'This is how everyone will recognise that you are my disciples — when they see the love you have for each other'
(John 13:35 *The Message*)

8. Task/Question (By yourself)
Think again about your own relationship — or lack of it — with the Christian church. Is there a branch of it near you where the love between the members demonstrates that they are followers of Christ?

*

Section 9

It is clear from the emphasis of Biblical texts as a whole, as well as our instinctive sense of what is appropriate, that this last requirement for the church — that of mutual love — is more important than all of the rest put together. Love is not only and end in itself but it is the medium in which the learning required can take place; it is the medium in which forgiveness of faults and mistakes can flourish; it is the medium in which challenges can be made and received without offence; it is the medium in which appreciation of each other's contributions can bloom; it is the medium which allows the full roundedness of Christ's character to be demonstrated and it is the medium in which God's goodness can be celebrated in shared worship.

So where does this leave us with regard to the connection between the church and unbreakable hope? Again Matthew's gospel, in particular, offers a helpful way of thinking about the issue, and that is in the concept of 'the kingdom of God'. Interestingly, Jesus had much more to say about the kingdom of God or of heaven, than he did about the church. It was his own focus, in other words, which we could surely benefit from adopting. It might mean more to us to refer to it as 'the 'place' where God's rule prevails' or 'the 'place' where things are done according to God's character', that is, in a way in which there is no darkness at all.

This broadens out way beyond the boundaries of the church to wherever light is prevailing. It also excludes anything happening within the so-called church which is at variance with God's character. This concept of God's kingdom carries its own antivirus device because as soon as anything ceases to be light-filled, it automatically loses its harmony with God's character. This reality therefore is one on which unbreakable hope can depend. The point here is that we cannot lazily assume that anything bearing the name of Christian will automatically encourage hope, or conversely, we cannot, judgementally assume that anything not bearing the name of Christian cannot be hopeful. Thinking, discerning, testing, judging will always be required of us. There are no short cuts.

As a practical example for this chapter, I have chosen to write about a project which crosses the boundaries between the church and other 'places' where God's rule may prevail, in a way which can help us to see the need for true discernment, rather than depending uncritically on what people call themselves.

A Hope-filled International Project

Recently I heard about a project in the West Bank, one of the Palestinian parts of the Middle East, which has been dogged by apparently intractable problems for so many years. The project is called the Jenin Creative Cultural Centre and was opened by Yousef Awad Shelaby, who was a captain in the Palestinian police force until he took partial retirement and opened the centre in 2005. It is for children, mostly of secondary school age, whose regular schooling is finished by early afternoon.

Because of the trouble in the Middle East, social activities for children have been severely curtailed, and they have nothing to do in their out-of-school hours and nowhere safe to go. At the centre, lessons are offered in the oud — the Arab lute — guitar, keyboard, violin, traditional Arab dancing, art and English. Yousef — along with other public sector workers — has not received his police pay for several months, and the centre is financed only through donations from agencies and individuals outside the country. For one English course offered by the centre to students of Al Quds University in Jerusalem, a small charge is made, as the students have some money, but for all the school children, courses are offered free of charge.

I heard of this project when my nephew, Charlie, was asked

by someone in an Edinburgh church with which he has strong connections, whether he would like to spend a part of his gap year as a volunteer in the Jenin centre. This Edinburgh church was giving financial support to the centre and felt that sending a worker, even for a short time, might be welcomed by Yousef. It turned out that this was the case, and I myself read some of Yousef's emails on the subject, in which he welcomed first the idea, and later Charlie himself, in the warmest possible terms. One he wrote to my sister, Charlie's mother, during Charlie's stay, reads as follows:

> 'I must thank you for the great gift you sent us (Charlie). You sent us the most lovely thing for you, to stay with us, which gives a wonderful impact on us and all the people who came to the centre; you can't imagine how much Charlie is a popular character and lovely one...From my deep heart all thanks'

What they wanted most from Charlie, who had been prepared to offer whatever he could, was the teaching of English lessons. Although Charlie had only just left school, he was able to take up the challenge, largely by offering English conversation sessions to children of various ages, one student group, and — most interesting of all — a group of Palestinian policemen. He also helped Yousef with the wording of funding applications in English, taught some guitar lessons to individuals and gave a presentation about Scotland, in which there seemed to be considerable interest. His skateboarding exploits were also much admired!

I'm sure the hope-filled aspects of this project will be evident in general, but one of the elements I find most significant about it is the reminder — if we need one — that the operation of the kingdom of God is by no means confined to the church, but can be seen wherever people act in accordance with the loving spirit of Christ to take an initiative that benefits their own community. Yousef is a Muslim who saw the needs of the children living in the refugee camp in Jenin, created as a result of the displacements caused by war and took steps to meet those needs even though he was suffering shortages himself.

9. Task/Question (Group/By yourself)
Look at a quality newspaper which has a good international section and work out approximately what percentage of the reports and features in it deal with good news, what percentage with bad and what percentage are simply neutral. Consider the reasons for your findings

and whether the proportions of good and bad news in the paper are a true reflection of what is happening in the world as a whole.

Section 10

Charlie was very struck by the way that life in the West Bank is like that of a developing country, whereas life in Israel is like that of a wealthy western country. There is a level of poverty in a place like Jenin which we might find hard, for example furnishings in the houses are rather sparse, many of the houses themselves are poor and there is not a great choice of shops, although food is good and plentiful.

Other aspects of life there which we might find tough include factors arising from the occupation, such as a relentless system of checkpoints where armed Israeli soldiers prolong unnecessary questioning and make what would normally be short easy journeys into marathons. It is usually a little easier for 'internationals' as visitors are called, but locals often have to take back roads and roundabout routes, leaving every vehicle at a checkpoint and finding another for the next leg of the journey. There is a prohibition on travel out of the West Bank for most of the inhabitants and everyday administrative tasks are made difficult if not impossible by the occupation. This results in many hardships and shortages, almost unbearable levels of frustration and a deep sense of injustice. It is also dangerous to be out after midnight as Israeli soldiers are patrolling the streets. There are occasional bursts of gunfire and sometimes trouble at the refugee camp in Jenin.

Other 'hardships' from Charlie's perspective, arose from the fact that Jenin is a rather conservative community and young boys and girls do not mix freely together or go to clubs in the evenings. The other side of that coin, however, is that one does not spend as much money, and that there is no violence on the streets arising from binge drinking. In fact, Charlie said he felt safer there than on the streets of Edinburgh for that reason. In general, although the occupation is a constant concern for the Palestinians, their levels of cheerfulness and hospitality are high, considering their circumstances. There is a rich social life and many busy coffee shops.

Although he could never have done so on the West Bank without being considered a collaborator, when he was travelling about in Israel, Charlie struck up conversations with young Israeli soldiers on a few occasions and discovered that many of them disliked the compulsory national service which they found themselves doing.

Most of the Israeli army presence in the occupied territories is made up of professional soldiers, however.

Charlie felt that although the political situation does not seem to show signs of resolving hopefully, the centre itself is a hope-filled place with purposeful activity of many kinds, workshops, plays and many international visitors such as Mairead Maguire, the Nobel peace prize winner from Northern Ireland who shared her perspective with Yousef and his team. Many of the children attending are having their education, and lives generally, greatly enhanced by what happens there.

Charlie himself certainly benefited hugely from his months in the centre. Besides the obvious boost to his confidence provided by managing to live alone and deal with a certain amount of loneliness in a largely non-English-speaking context, he took a leaf out of the Muslim book by trying to pray specifically five times a day, though not wishing to use set prayers as Muslims do.

He was impressed by the Arab culture: the music of the oud, the savoury food, the unbelievably generous hospitality. He admired Yousef and several of the other teachers at the centre and made friends there. He returned with a much clearer idea of what he would like to study and with a desire to return when he is better qualified in both teaching English as a foreign language and in Arabic. Towards the end of his stay in Jenin, he wrote the following in an email home:

> 'I am increasingly thinking that I would like to come back. ... I want to help more in Palestine, teaching or other. Maybe I can study Arabic.'

His understanding of the Palestinian plight is much greater than it was, yet he sees something of the Israeli point of view too. He encountered some resistance and some lack of comprehension about his desire to volunteer in Jenin, both from pro-Jewish volunteers and Scottish friends and had an opportunity to work out his own views about the whole situation. It has been a truly life-changing experience for him.

At the time of this study going to press, Charlie has completed a qualification in teaching English as a foreign language and is in the process of studying Arabic at university. He has visited the centre several more times and taken some of his fellow Arabic students there too, who have been able to offer various courses to the children. It is an association which continues to be mutually beneficial.

10. Task/Question (Group/By yourself)

Identify an international project that you would like to take an interest in, and start collecting information about it. See what aspects of it stir up your desire to pray, give or otherwise participate in it.

Chapter 4: 'Rest for the People of God'

Section 1

In this chapter I would like to consider the 'content' of unbreakable hope. So far we have been noting that it is unbreakable because it is based on the light-filled character of God. I am not forgetting that for some readers, this is still being accepted as an experiment and an exploration. We have also been clearing the ground of false hopes and the distractions that may draw us away from true hope and lead to disillusionment. I would like to return now to a statement I made in section 8 of chapter 2, and that is: 'Jesus has already finished God's work of restoring everything, ourselves included'.*

The last words Jesus spoke on the cross included the statement, 'It is finished.'(John 19:30) or as *The Message* has it: 'It's done... complete.' Earlier in John, (17:4) Jesus spoke in a prayer to the Father of 'completing down to the last detail what you assigned me to do.' Then after his death, resurrection and ascension, Jesus is shown by the writer of Hebrews (for example in10:12+ff), sitting at the right hand of God where

> 'he waits for his enemies to be made his footstool, because by one sacrifice he has made perfect for ever those who are being made holy.'(*NIV*)

Just as God the Father rested after creating the world and seeing that it was good, Jesus is now resting at the right hand of God after having redeemed the world by his totally effective work of self sacrifice. The people of God likewise are called into rest by the writer of Hebrews. This rest is far more than simply keeping the Sabbath or refraining from work on Sundays which is still argued about legalistically in some parts of the church. It is a call

---

* *I owe a great debt in the understanding of this issue and all the benefits it brings to an exposition of parts of the book of Hebrews given by Alan Richardson during a course of lectures about thirty years ago in the town of Hawick in the Scottish Borders. The truths he expounded then have really stood the test of time and have been quite life-changing for me and a constant source of inspiration. While acknowledging that debt, I wish to take full responsibility for the re-expression of them now, as I have absorbed and worked them out in my own experience.*

to a rest of spirit which is secured by the conviction that Jesus' work truly has restored all things to their true and rightful state.

If we look at the quotation from Hebrews above, we see various different timescales mentioned. 'He has made perfect for ever' refers to what has already been done. 'Those who are being made holy' refers to a process which is presently happening, and 'He waits' refers to something which is to come in future. Christ himself exercises a hope which consists of an expectation that his enemies will be completely subdued. In other words, all that is wrong will be made right. This encompasses more than we are even capable of imagining, and this is where the Holy Spirit comes to our aid. In 1 Corinthians 2: 9-10 *(NIV)* Paul says:

> 'No eye has seen, no ear has heard, no mind has conceived what God has prepared for those who love him- but God has revealed it to us by his Spirit.'

and:

> 'We have not received the spirit of the world but the Spirit who is from God, that we may understand what God has freely given us.'
> (1 Corinthians 2:12 *NIV*)

1. Task/Question (By yourself)
Consider a field of human activity with which you are familiar (education, health, family life, entertainment — anything) and spend some time imagining what it would be like if all that is wrong were to be made right. What will this field of activity be like in 'the new earth'? Ask the Holy Spirit to inform your reflections.
*

Section 2

Are you the sort of person who, when reading a book or watching a film full of unbearable suspense, can't rest until you have sneaked a look at the ending to see if everything turns out all right? Do you find yourself sometimes paralysed by anxiety and unable to decide on a course of action because too much hangs on the outcome? Can you at least sympathise with such attitudes? These concerns are often those of a person with a lively imagination who does not need to be warned of possible dangers because he or she is only too aware of what might go wrong in a given situation.

Someone suffering from this sort of acute anxiety needs to be aware also of Jesus' position of rest at the right hand of the Father where he waits in complete confidence for 'his enemies to be made his footstool'. Consider also the picture of Jesus asleep in the boat while the disciples panic that they will be drowned in the storm. This vision of restful trust is also pictured in the well-known novel, 'To Kill a Mockingbird' by Harper Lee. The two children Jem and Scout watch their father Atticus to see if it's time to be anxious. If he is calm, they relax, because they know he is trustworthy.

The art of this sort of rest is indeed a matter of learning to look at our God in a crisis rather than looking at the crisis itself. Again it is a change of focus. It is not the kind of rest that necessarily means inactivity, although that may sometimes be required, but rather that any activity undertaken in this restful attitude will be to the purpose and not rash or damaging. The reason is that it will be undertaken in the unbreakable hope that God's enemies are being 'made his footstool' on the basis of what Christ has done and not on the basis of what we ourselves have done or not done.

One of the most prevalent problems in our society today is that of uncontrolled or excessive stress. Millions of work hours are lost because of stress related illness and thousands of courses are delivered on stress management. Many people spend ridiculous numbers of hours at work at the expense of their family life or their health or both and others feel that everything hangs on them in a really burdensome way. Their lives have become a long dark tunnel in which brief periods of respite are only used to recover sufficient energy for a return to the fray. Many people lie awake at night worrying about what they have to do and feeling quite unable to do it. They feel the nightmare of full responsibility combined with an inability to change anything. We have to understand that such a spirit does not come from God in whom there is no darkness at all. Therefore we have every right to repudiate it utterly.

2. Task/Question (Group)
Read Hebrews 4:9-11 in the *NIV*. Try to express what these verses might mean in your own way in vocal or written form. Also read the last paragraph of Matthew 11 in *The Message* (verses 28-30) and imagine that these words are being spoken to you personally by God himself.

*

Section 3

The essential point in all of this is that our unbreakable hope lies in who Christ is and what Christ has done. This has happened already and no amount of error or messing up on our own part can ever undo it. Our failures and sins, though often dire and terrible in nature, can never compete in powerful effectiveness with the unshakable love and saving action of God himself as expressed in the person of Christ. This is why our hope is unbreakable — it has already been guaranteed by the one in whom there is no darkness at all. This is why all fretting and anxiety can be laid aside and peace of mind embraced. It is not a case of closing our eyes to reality, but a case of focussing on a deeper reality. No matter what is happening on the surface of our lives — and it can be, and sometimes is, very painful, perplexing or horrifying — the deeper reality is unchanged, though not untouched, by our griefs and problems.

Why then, in view of such a situation, do we continue in stress and anxiety so much of the time? Why is it so difficult to lay down our fretting and fuming and move into the peace of God which has been opened up to us by Christ's actions?

One way of explaining it, to some degree, is to think of how children try to master an activity which may be new to them but which has been done successfully many times by their parents. Sometimes they are willing to accept help or instruction, to learn peacefully, being unphased by their own mistakes, persevering until they achieve the success appropriate to their stage of development. At other times they may refuse all offers of help, insisting on doing it themselves, even though it may be evident to a more experienced person that their efforts are doomed because of some basic mistake or misunderstanding which will certainly result in failure. They may resent intervention of any sort and be devastated by their failure, refusing all consolation and reassurance. Their feelings at such a time can best be summed up by the sentence: '*I* want to do it *myself*'.

This analogy is not entirely satisfactory because a child learning a new skill does reach a point at which it is quite appropriate for him to do the action without help from anyone else. However, what we are considering here is the action of redeeming the whole world — or at least a whole field of activity — from disaster, and it is quite amazing how we so readily assume that it all depends on our own efforts. We may not realise that we are appropriating such a pivotal role to ourselves in any given situation, but human pride and self-importance are so seductive that whenever we feel ourselves to be suffering unbearable stress, it is almost certain that we have overstepped our own proper area of responsibility and are trying to 'play God' in some way.

3. Task/Question (By yourself)

Think back to the last time you felt very overburdened by some responsibility you believed was yours. Reconsider the issue with the advantage of distance. Was it really your responsibility? Had someone else given you that impression? Were there aspects of the situation that honestly were outside your control and outside your remit?

*

Section 4

Humility is the gateway out of stress. That's why we will sometimes do anything other than take it. This is one aspect of the 'narrow way' to life which Jesus spoke of. It is a way we will only consider when we have broken ourselves trying to do it all ourselves and seriously entertained the idea of becoming tragic or self-pitying in our failure. When we have reached such a point, there is sometimes a moment of grace in which we realise that we may lay down the load we have been carrying because we ourselves and the load we have been shouldering have both been given a lift by a huge powerful lorry which is taking us all in the right direction. Rest is the only logical response. We may feel a little foolish for having thought it was all up to us, but the primary feeling is — quite rightly — massive relief.

This discovery needs to be guarded very carefully, as it will be attacked again and again by people who have refused the narrow way and therefore have a vested interest in discrediting it. Such people have themselves undertaken very stressful activities and — to put it crudely — want the credit for having done so. Perhaps they should be given such credit, but it is not the way of the unbreakable hope we are studying; at any time the stress they are enduring could break them so there is an essential insecurity about such an enterprise. It is only as strong as the person undertaking it.

If God himself is the centre and his concerns are the ones we wish to embrace, then his is the ultimate responsibility for any enterprise we may have undertaken in obedience to him. The service we offer is like that of a child who is serving his father. The father is always there and is taking full responsibility for the project. The child may not be able to conceive of the finished project in its entirety, but is at peace because his father knows what he is doing and even if things appear to the child to be going wrong, he does not become over-responsible and anxious. He simply watches with interest to see what his father will do, either to sort things out or to show that they have not actually gone off track at all. He will do this even if others come along and make disparaging remarks about the project or express doubts or even criticisms of him. The only way he can be thrown is if he begins to doubt that his father does know what he is doing, or in other words, if he begins to believe that there is actually some 'darkness' in his father.

To carry the analogy further, the time will come when the father will have trained the child in certain aspects of the project and will be able to leave it up to the child to complete a section of the work without constant supervision. Because the child has seen it done many times and done it under supervision many times, he will tackle the task with confidence, knowing he can consult if necessary. If he tackles something he has not been asked to do, however, he may get into difficulties or do damage to himself or others. This highlights the other danger that threatens us — that of going off in an independent direction for reasons of our own, instead of sticking to our proper field of operation.

4. Task/Question (By yourself)
Can you identify an activity of your own which you believed was within your rightful field of operation, but where doubt crept in to disable you? Now try to identify an activity which you undertook but which was really outside your proper remit and so came unstuck.

*

Section 5

One of the reasons we may undertake an enterprise which is too much for us, is the understandable and even praiseworthy desire to make a significant contribution to the lives of others and our own or to leave our mark in some way upon the environment in which we live. Where such a desire can come adrift is if instead of being truly altruistic, it becomes an attempt to prove ourselves in some way — in other words, it springs from insecurity instead of faith. Other people can help us here, as it is usually clear to someone outside the enterprise whether it is being genuinely offered or being done to bring reassurance or glory to the one doing it. The spirit in which it is being done bears similar fruit in the recipients. If it is being done in a restful spirit they will be blessed by it, but if there is striving and struggle of a self-interested nature, they will feel uneasy and uncomfortable about receiving it, or they may feel inferior and second rate by comparison, if they do not realise what is going on.

Another factor which can cause confusion in this connection is the influence of peer pressure. If we do not have the priorities of God himself to guide us in what we undertake, we may easily look sideways at our colleagues or other companions to decide what and how much to undertake and in what way and at what speed. This 'one size fits all' approach can result in trying to work to someone else's agenda instead of finding our own proper rhythm of work and rest. Of course an employer is entitled to require certain hours of work and the successful completion of certain projects from his employees, but at the time of accepting such employment we need to be very aware of our gifts and limitations so that we do not sign up to something which is beyond us.

However, this is not usually the difficulty with overwork and stress. More often it arises from some self-imposed aspect of the task which we try to complete to prove our superiority to someone else or to prove to ourselves that we are the best or as good as someone else or not a failure, or any number of unworthy and often subconscious motives. The antidote to such strivings lies in the assurance that the ultimate responsibility lies with God himself and that he has finished his work already. The heat is off; the pressure is relaxed; the intensity is dispelled and the focus is removed from ourselves.

When this pressure is lifted we can then be free to listen to the inner promptings of the 'still small voice' and find the true motivation from within, the genuine desire to do the task for the right reasons. We can remember why we wanted to do it in the first place and see the thing in proportion. If you know you are susceptible to the temptation to become a workaholic, do not be surprised if you are rendered incapable of doing anything at all for some periods of time until you remember that the responsibility for the project does not lie with you. As Milton said in the sonnet *On his Blindness*:

'God doth not need
Either man's work or his own gifts, who best
Bear his mild yoke, they serve him best, his state

Is kingly. Thousands at his bidding speed
And post o'er land and ocean without rest.
  They also serve who only stand and wait'

5. Task/Question (Group)

Consider the proposition that who we are is more important to God than what we do.

*

Section 6

We have to decide: do we want to go through life involved in stressful dominance or restful participation? It's a loaded question because not one of us is equal to the position of dominance, so if we choose the former, we are doomed to failure. God himself is the only one who can sustain the position of control without collapse, yet because we cannot accept or believe that, he gives up all his power — to which he is fully entitled — and takes up a position of weakness, letting us try on the crown for size. The patience of God in this regard is quite amazing. He lets us embark on all sorts of impossible missions, knowing that we will only surrender to him when we realise how unable we are. This is such an unfashionable and unfamiliar way to think that it is a lesson most of us have to learn again and again.

The Bible is full of stories which emphasise this point, namely that the power of God is made perfect in weakness. Think of David and Goliath; think of Gideon being told to reduce his army to only three hundred men; think of the pitifully small meal of five loaves and two fish used to feed a great crowd. Perhaps the most amazing story of all is that of the great rescue of humankind being undertaken by a small-town artisan who was executed for presuming to be God himself and only leaving eleven, rather wavering, followers to spread the news. The very fact that millions now build their lives on the work of this person is testimony to its efficacy against all likelihood. The first of the beatitudes — the sayings of Jesus in one of his early sermons — is:

'Blessed are the poor in spirit, for theirs is the kingdom of heaven'. (Matthew 5:3 *NIV*)

The Message version reads:

'You're blessed when you're at the end of your rope. With less of you there is more of God and his rule'.

In a world which admires power and strength, we must maintain our position that the only true strength is God's. Any other is limited and temporary at best, and false and misleading at worst. This is another way of saying that only God is God and we are his creatures. Once we have understood this, the resources of that heavenly power can be opened up to us in an astounding way.

When Moses had tried to save the Israelites by his own efforts and only succeeded in discrediting himself with them, he ran away from the whole thing and spent many years in the desert: a nobody. Then came the call to do the very thing he had resolved not to touch and in a way, he was still taken up with his past failure. He did not realise that such self-knowledge was the very thing which qualified him to be used by God as he was in no danger of thinking he could do it all himself.

In the New Testament, the apostle Peter believed and claimed that he would stick by Jesus to the death, but Jesus warned him that he would not be able to do this. Only when Peter realised what he was like was Jesus able to give him the task of leadership in the young church. Both Moses and Peter had to go by the way of humility but both became great men of faith in their different ways, once they knew that the mode of operating in God's kingdom is not by superhuman feats of strength and endurance, but by resting in what God has done, is doing and will do.

6. Task/Question (By yourself)

Think back to a time when you felt you failed terribly. Perhaps you can hardly bear to think about it still. Then put this issue into the context of the experiences of Moses (murder) and Peter (denial). Ask yourself how your self-knowledge has increased as a result of your failure. Then listen to what God may be asking of you, in your changed state.

*

Section 7

There is a joy in this restful way of operating. Each time you experience the effective working of God in your situation, your certainty about the hope we have will be strengthened. Also, you will be freer to undertake tasks you are given, knowing that if you have honestly been given the task in question, the responsibility for it and the power by which it is to be done belong to God himself. At the same time, if you appropriate improper control of the situation, you know it may go very wrong, so humility is your only — but your unbreakable — hope.

You will also be freer to refuse tasks which are not part of your proper remit as you know that God's purposes will not be served by them, however apparently successful they may look. People operating in true rest may seem to be out of step with those around them. They may even seem to be lazy or irresponsible, but the things they touch will have a security and an economy about them. They will not necessarily be the most outwardly successful, but their work will generate soundness in the institutions and environments in which they operate. Others will come to expect value and rightness in their vicinity. Because they are resting on the power of God, they can feel free to take in what is happening to the people round about them and to relate to that in appropriate ways.

As well as joy in this way of functioning, there is a sense of adventure. Things are not predictable or boring. There is an element of unexpectedness, of freshness. Work undertaken in this spirit generates life and a sense of discovery. This aspect of surprise springs from the fact that a person operating in rest is operating in liaison with the Holy Spirit, and is not controlling the whole thing for himself. It is a joint venture and therefore has the dynamic of a relationship about it. There will be constant conversation — prayer — about the progress of the work and about how it should proceed. Successes, problems and developments can be analysed and decisions taken in tandem. It is essentially an interesting way to live.

If you are in contact for a period of time with a person who operates in the spirit of rest, and then you are separated from him or her, you will find upon renewed contact, that he or she will have moved on in subtle ways from the place at which you left him or her. There will not be a sameness or a staleness; there will be a sense of progress. Of course it is only too possible to stop resting on God at any time and to start striving and toiling again, but once you have experienced the rest of God you will remember it and seek to return to it as soon as you realise you have left it. You will get better at spotting the moment when you start to struggle and deciding not to go there.

7. Task/Question (By yourself)

Think back to a time when you experienced the restful way of living described above. Make sure you can identify that sense of peaceful progress in your own experience and tell yourself that this is what God has given you. Look up Hebrews 4:9-11 for back-up.

*

Section 8

There is another area in which we are in dire need of God's rest and that is in connection with our own progress as individuals. This is especially true of aspects of our behaviour which we have already become convinced are all wrong and need to be changed. Sometimes these areas become hotbeds of struggle and shame, or targets of New Year resolutions or special drives or efforts. However, these areas are just as subject to the principles of rest as any other. Again it is a question of relinquishing the wrong sort of control over these issues and accepting ourselves at the stage we may have reached in any matter. It does not mean accepting unacceptable behaviour in ourselves or anyone else. Rather, it means realising that Christ himself believes that what is unacceptable has been given a fatal blow as a result of what he has done and that it is in the process of being brought under his authority in those who belong to him. We are not 'the finished article'. This again requires humility. I have to acknowledge that I am not yet the way I want to be. However, part of my unbreakable hope is that I will become increasingly like Christ himself as I continue to rest in his achievements and to co-operate with his workings.

Something I have noticed is that what I think needs to be changed most about myself is not necessarily Christ's priority for me. If you have had any sort of dealings with a teenager who is worried about his or her self image, you will appreciate that such a person can be acutely distressed about some aspect of his or her appearance when to you, he or she seems to be the very picture of youthful freshness and appeal. You may wish, in such a case, that the person could glimpse themselves as you see them for a second, and see how unnecessary their distress is. This gives a pale reflection of how Christ sees us, for whom he has given himself, and how he wants to give us a glimpse of ourselves as he sees us. Work that still needs to be done on us is his responsibility and to be effective, must be tackled in a spirit of rest and trust, not in one of menace, fearfulness or despair. It is also to be seen within the context of his love for us and of his work of redemption *that has already been done and paid for.* This is difficult to receive because we have to admit our need.

Peter was ashamed about Jesus washing his feet because he had not yet realised that he would deny Jesus. He still believed that he would be able to follow him to the death. Then, when Jesus explained that only those whose feet he washed would have any part with him, Peter went to the other extreme and wanted his hands and head to be washed as well, underestimating the progress he had already made in his friendship with Christ. Essentially, Peter wanted to control that friendship, rather than be open to its natural unfolding, which is the way of trust. Only after the experience of denying his beloved friend, was Peter able to be restored by being given the chance to express his loyalty from a position of real self-knowledge. (John 21:15+ff) Our progress is Christ's responsibility. We participate in it rather than controlling it.

8. Task/Question (By yourself)

Try to identify an area of your own life where you are exercised about your own progress. If you feel you can, decide to yield control to Christ and resolve to be at peace about it and participate restfully in developments there, resisting the temptation to judge yourself harshly.

*

Section 9

A Hope-filled Church Choir Project

A well-loved verse in Zechariah 4 contains a message for the benefit of the Israelites who had returned from exile in Babylon and were undertaking the rebuilding of the Temple in Jerusalem in difficult and adverse circumstances. It reads:

'Not by might nor by power, but by my Spirit,' says the Lord Almighty.' (Zech. 4:6 *NIV*)

This verse is particularly relevant to the issue of rest which we have been considering, as it emphasises the point that human strength is not the agency by which important progress is made in the spiritual realm.

The verse also provided the title of a CD of worship prepared by a church choir of which I was a member for a while. I would like to tell you the story of the production of 'By the Spirit', as it seems to me to have been a good example of something undertaken in the spirit of restful trust outlined above.

The project was suggested to us because of the positive response of the congregation to the songs and hymns we were in the habit of singing as they gathered for worship on a Sunday morning. The choir was in very good heart at the time, being a group of ten people of different ages, led from the keyboard by Olwen, and beginning to tackle four-part harmony in some pieces as well as having some guitar-accompanied folk song tunes and some Gaelic songs in our repertoire. We sometimes used other instruments as well. There was a sense among us all of being privileged to be in the group at the time and a sense also of the blessing of God resting on us and going out to others as we sang. Several of those who heard us sing asked if we would think of making a CD of some of our favourites and this idea took root.

Then, early in 2005, Olwen, looking for ways of improving the quality of the music for Sunday worship, suggested we should aim to buy an organ specifically designed to accompany voices and suited to church use, and that for this purpose, we might take up the idea of making a recording, the proceeds of which could be used for a suitable organ. The idea was approved by the choir who felt a percentage of the profits should go to a chosen charity and we obtained the consent of the Kirk Session. Then I spoke to Will, who was skilled in recording music at the local college where he taught a traditional music course.

The cost was going to be about £2000 and of course this would be required before any monies for the CDs themselves came in. At this point, Donnie, our guitarist, remembered a trust fund which awarded small grants for Christian projects and discovered that their next meeting was imminent. He and Olwen and I put together an application asking for 60% of the recording costs and our application was considered immediately and positively, the trust fund awarding us £1200 just before Christmas 2005. This result, together with the sense of shared responsibility for the project, encouraged us tremendously and later in 2006, we arranged a 'Big Sing', a musical evening of the kind we had done before, in order to raise the rest of the funds needed and to launch the CD. In this, the congregation was very supportive and the other funds were forthcoming, with hard work certainly, but without a sense of strain.

9. Task/Question (Group)
Can you identify a project or activity which you have been involved in where the door seemed simply to open in this way? Try to analyse the reasons for this sense of 'flow'.

*

Section 10

By this time, our congregation was going through a fairly lengthy and problematical vacancy and the choir project and weekly singing generated a sense of ongoing church life at a time when it was badly needed: 'A sense of togetherness — a real sense of worship, an awareness of the presence of God', as one of the ministers doing long-term pulpit supply put it. Our actual recording sessions took place on three different Saturdays during the winter of 2006, when Will brought his portable recording equipment to our church hall, which provided an excellent recording studio. Olwen and others of us selected twelve of the songs and hymns that had particularly blessed us all and we worked hard, but again with a sense of purpose and ease, to make the recording as musical as possible in the time we had. Will was very helpful in his use of the equipment, to correct mistakes and to lay instrumental tracks on top of the singing where required. These were happy days for us and the final version of the CD when Will had prepared the pre-master, represented our best efforts, not perfect by any means, but a good sound on the whole, and carrying something of the blessing we had experienced when doing it.

Thereafter, some of us prepared the sleeve which was illustrated by a local artist and carried the words of the songs. Finally the finished article was sent off to a company who produced the 500 copies just in time for the 'Big Sing' mentioned above, before the summer holidays 2006, the whole project having been completed within about a year. Thereafter, distribution and sales could proceed over the next few months and warm, positive feedback began to come in both locally and from further afield as people began to listen to and benefit from the worship on the CD. Some of the unsolicited comments were:

'A salve for the soul', 'soothing and uplifting', 'the words and music have calmed, encouraged and uplifted me over the past months when I have sometimes been very low in spirit', 'it is refreshing, unpretentious and clear. You have a good range of different styles of material and a very pleasant tone/blend of voices', 'the choir, the singing, was an inspiration to me and kept my spirit alive during a time when I was scared'. Of course these comments and others like them encouraged the choir very much and confirmed the sense we had had all along of being engaged in something which was inspired and enabled by the Spirit of God.

By February 2007, our target amount of £5000 had been reached and the choir as a group made a trip to Edinburgh to look at and order the organ and to sing in a couple of congregations who had invited us to do so. The trip was very enjoyable and carried a sense of the fulfilment of the whole project. A few weeks later, the father and son team from the Organ Studio came up to instal the new organ in its place, where it is regularly used for Sunday worship, as planned. When the CDs were all sold there was enough to make a donation to Tear Fund which represented 10% of the total raised and made a fitting conclusion to the whole undertaking.

10. Task/Question (Group/By yourself)

Conduct an experiment in this way of operating by tackling what seems to be suggesting itself to you as a positive task. It should be both something you really want to do and something which others will benefit from.

Chapter 5: Human Freedom: its Value and its Cost

Section 1

We have been spending some time clearing away obstacles to true hope which may crop up in connection with the church, but for many people these pale into insignificance when compared to hindrances to hope in the world as a whole. In chapter 1, I touched on this issue in the ninth section and its question and we shall revisit it in this chapter at greater length.

In many ways, this is the heart of the matter, because there is no escaping the terrible aspects of life in this world; especially it seems for vulnerable people such as the very young, the very old, the very ill, the very poor, the very weak. Even for those who are not in these categories, there are heartaches aplenty in their own circumstances, for example in the breakdown of health or relationships, in loss, accident or grief. There is no need for more to be said as we all know this only too well, and the older we are, the clearer it is to us that something is horribly wrong with the world. If we are fortunate for the moment, we have daily evidence that others are not. How can unbreakable hope help us here?

First of all, we cannot, as some have tried to do, pretend that 'it's not as bad as all that', that if we only adopt a positive outlook, we can magic away the ills of the world. Such an attempt results in belittling the suffering of others, or even our own and can have the effect of taking us into unreality and insincerity — essentially an avoidance mechanism, rightly criticised by those who wish to be honest about their own and others' experiences. In other words, an excruciating pain is an excruciating pain, whatever its cause and whatever we think its purpose may be. An attempt to alleviate it is the only humane reaction for anyone with an iota of compassion.

That said, we also need to look into possible causes and purposes, so that we may either avoid the pain in future or at least be able to endure it without also having a sense that it is meaningless. With regard to the pain of others, finding a cause may also enable prevention and/ or cure, and finding a purpose may enable encouragement. Whatever we do, an active response is required: to alleviate, to prevent, to support another who is struggling with pain or hardship and perhaps a mixture of all three. Wringing our hands on the sidelines is to waste the compassion we feel. That is not to say, of course, that effecting substantial help will necessarily be easy. One of the worst aspects of the suffering of the people of Burma, for example, was that the oppressive regime would not allow free access to aid agencies who wished to bring help to those devastated by the cyclone.

This example is instructive because it illustrates two at least of the causes of such a catastrophe. One is the natural event of the cyclone causing devastation, and the other is the desire of the oppressive regime for power at all costs, both the natural world and the human one causing terrible suffering to many people. It may also be that human activity has had some effect on the frequency and severity of the cyclones, as those investigating global warming suggest.

1. Task/Question (Group)
Read Mark 6:35-44, one of the accounts of the feeding of the five thousand. How did Jesus address the sense of helplessness the disciples felt in the face of enormous need? What principle can we draw from the amount of money the disciples reckoned would be needed and the smallness of what they actually had?

*

Section 2

Many people are convinced of the need for all of us to do what we can in the face of terrible suffering and few would now try to argue that it is God's will, or worse, his punishment for wrongdoing, that certain people seem to have so little going for them, but there remains the old question: if God is all powerful, why does he not step in and rearrange circumstances in favour of the unfortunate? How does the state of affairs in this world square with a God in whom there is no darkness at all?

Another look at the feeding of the five thousand may be useful here, because after Jesus was offered the little meal:

'looking up to heaven, he gave thanks and broke the loaves. Then he gave them to his disciples to set before the people. He also divided the two fish among them all. They all ate and were satisfied.' (Mark 6:41-42 *NIV*)

If that isn't divine intervention, what is it? Set aside for a moment, all the other 'ifs and buts' that naturally come to mind, and consider what happened on this occasion:

> The disciples identified a need and wanted Jesus to do something about it.
>
> Jesus told them to meet the need themselves.
>
> They said they couldn't do it.
>
> He asked them what they *could* do.
>
> They worked out what they could offer.
>
> Jesus told them to prepare the people to receive what they needed.
>
> *Jesus took what was offered, thanked God and broke the loaves and fish.*
>
> *He gave the gift back to the disciples and instructed them to distribute it.*
>
> *The need was fully met and there was plenty left over.*

What, I wonder, was the content of Jesus' prayer of thanks? What was he so thankful to God for? Was it the five loaves and the two fish? Was it the willingness to give and the faith in him shown by the boy whose loaves and fish they were? (John's gospel is the only one to tell us of the donor specifically — chapter 6, verse 9.) Was it the opportunity to meet the need of the crowd by using the offering and actions of his followers? Was it the chance to show his followers how their little could be made more than enough? Was it the chance to show his followers who he was?

Why did Jesus go through this elaborate procedure outlined by all four gospel writers? Why not command food to fall from the skies if he had that sort of power? It is clear he deliberately involved his followers in the miracle and that he delighted to share the act of generosity and compassion with them. He seemed to be encouraging them to draw the mercy of God down into a mundane situation by giving what they had and trusting God to turn it into more than enough. It is another example of his desire to share his divine creative power, which we noted earlier in chapter 4.

I know that for some people this begs all sorts of questions — about the authority of scripture at the very least — but we are not reliant only on that for the soundness of the principle illustrated here. Many people who have embarked on a mission of mercy without having the resources to fulfil it can testify to that: for example Yusuf, who opened the centre in Jenin, described in chapter 3, or Iain MacAskill who pioneered the An Caladh Centre, described in chapter 2. There are other, more famous examples, such as Dr. Barnardo opening his orphanages, Gladys Aylward taking children to safety during a war and so on. We probably all have our favourite stories of brave people reaching out to fulfil a dire need and praying effectively that provision would be made for them. We are surely meant to do more than simply admire them.

2. Task/Question (Group/By yourself)

Do you have it in you to turn your compassion for the suffering of others into substantial help, even though you do not think you have the resources to do so? Spend some time thinking about this and be prepared to start small if you are not yet engaged in something of this kind.

*

Section 3

Hope Home

'Hope Home', a Tanzanian orphanage, is an example of how this can happen. The story was recounted to me by my friend Lucy who belongs to a church in Brighton of about sixty members. (Names of people have been changed to preserve confidentiality.)

It began with a young girl called Rita, of white and Caribbean parentage. When she first came to take the Alpha course — an introduction to the Christian faith — being run by the Brighton church, Rita was seventeen years old and a quiet, shy girl. She gradually grew in confidence and began to find out what she thought God wanted for her life. When the Alpha course finished, Rita joined a monthly meeting called Alpha Plus, a group for Bible study, prayer and mutual support where various older women took a concerned interest in her progress. They gradually began to realise what huge confidence her faith had given her — 'a Spirit-given, God-directed boldness', as one of them described it.

Rita began to feel certain that she should go to Africa and found a church link with an Assemblies of God church which was conducting missions in Tanzania, a largely Moslem country. She took part in these missions, finding to her amazement that when she preached the gospel, people responded and difficult situations were turned around.

It seems that a task had been waiting for Rita in the town of Moshi in Tanzania. A number of years ago, a Swedish nurse — not a Christian — had been working closely with a Tanzanian pastor, his wife Elizabeth and their son John. When John grew up he ran an orphanage and did some preaching in the church. This pastor died and the Swedish nurse returned to Sweden but later, sent money to 'Mama Elizabeth' who had always wanted her own orphanage for Aids orphans. Mama Elizabeth was also praying for a wife for her son John and had a dream of the girl he would marry. A few days later, Rita arrived in Moshi and Elizabeth recognised the girl in her dream, but wisely did not say anything about it. John's aunt, however, who was dying, spoke to John and Rita, put Rita's hand in that of John and said they were meant for one another. At first Rita was doubtful about this but after she returned to the UK, she reconsidered, and to cut a long story short, went back to Tanzania and married John.

Soon, Mama Elizabeth and Rita started their own orphanage in Moshi. They rented both land and a house opposite Mama Elizabeth's house, using the funds sent by the Swedish nurse, and ten children arrived quickly to take up the places. They were from Christian homes having been referred to their pastor and then to Mama Elizabeth. Eight of the ten were Aids orphans and there were some siblings among them. They called the orphanage 'Hope Home', using the word 'home' rather than 'house' as some of the youngest children did not know they were orphans and Rita felt the word 'home' was so much closer to what they wanted for the children than 'orphanage'. The Brighton church decided to support the work of Hope Home.

3. Task/Question (Group)

Consider the way this decision to support Hope Home came about. In what way is it a good illustration of the saying that 'Charity begins at home'?

*

Section 4

When she was expecting her second child, Rita returned to the UK, visited the Alpha Plus group and updated them about the children in Hope Home. Some of them were very traumatised by their previous experiences and did things like hiding food in their beds. Swedish funds pay for the running of the home — rent, food, the school fees of the school-aged children and salaries for a guard and male and female workers. Mama Elizabeth and Rita look after the pre-school children as well as Rita's own two.

The Tanzanian government has a policy that orphans who are HIV positive should live separately from those who are not, so all the children were tested accordingly and all were clear. One of the youngest orphans, Ebrahim, who had seemed very disturbed, was not there on the day of the test and when he was three years old, developed the tell-tale lesions on his body. Mama Elizabeth and Rita were very anxious that a vulnerable young boy should not suffer the further trauma of being separated from everything familiar and they prayed hard for him. At home, members of the Brighton church also prayed that what the children had been told about Jesus would not be undercut by such a cruel separation. Mercifully, when he was finally tested, he was clear and so was able to stay at Hope Home to everyone's great relief and delight. His disturbed behaviour also died down as he adjusted to normal living.

The Alpha Plus group began to raise money as well as collecting items which would be useful to Hope Home. They organised a bake sale and used it as an excuse to give further information to the whole congregation about Rita and to mobilise support for the orphanage. On that occasion, an Italian girl who had wanted to work with children in Africa felt God was speaking to her about going to work with Rita and began to make plans to go.

Some of the Alpha Plus group organised fund-raisers such as healthy eating meals and discussed what else they could do. As well as asking their own congregation and friends, they invited the local school to take part. They discovered that a shop in Arusha — a town near Moshi — imported goods from the UK and the owners were willing to share some of their container to transport necessities to Hope Home. Bikes for the children, clothes, videos, old computers were collected and packed at Aldershot. The customs officials were very particular about how the goods were packed and the process had to be redone. People rallied to collect goods, a van was hired to drive to Aldershot, five people went there to repack and list all the items in the required way. The container was held up in Mombasa, because of riots there and it became a prayer project that the container should get safely to Arusha, which it eventually did and was received with much excitement.

Money was also sent by international bank transfer to Hope Home. There were administrative difficulties here too, as the orphanage was not yet registered because of problems in getting to Dar-es-Salaam where the business was to be transacted.

Rita and Mama Elizabeth wanted to be able to buy their own land to build an orphanage for twenty children and when the Brighton church had a 'Vision Night' they decided to adopt Rita as their Mission Partner and to set a target of raising £5000, the cost of the land required. When this was presented to the whole congregation, the money to be raised started flooding in. Some people organised cream teas, others opened their gardens and some simply gave from their own resources.

When Rita and John were in the UK for the birth of their second baby, they visited the Brighton church, reported on progress and were encouraged to look for land as the cost of it would be met by the Brighton church, which had by that time raised £1700 towards it.

Meanwhile, another friend of Lucy's, Frances, told Lucy that she had a friend Sam, an architect who had been involved in building orphanages in Uganda. Lucy looked up the relevant website and saw an ideal example of his work, a house for eight children and a house mother. She emailed Sam who was doing work in Dar-es-Salaam for the Salvation Army. Some time later, Sam and his wife visited their friend Frances in UK and Lucy was able to meet them. Sam said he would be looking for paid employment very soon and has been engaged to build the new orphanage for Hope Home.

As the money raised for Hope Home increased, it was necessary that a charitable trust be set up to administer it. Lucy consulted the Charities Commission and the clergy of the church and set up the trust accordingly. During the following four months or so, the rest of the money to buy the land was raised, even though the cost of the plot had almost doubled in that time. The money was sent, the plot bought and the building is due to begin.

As Lucy told me about this project, her excitement and enthusiasm were palpable as events seemed to be unfolding before her very eyes. Every step forward was cause for rejoicing and every obstacle was cause for prayer and imaginative response. Lucy noticed that she no longer felt fearful when things seemed to be going wrong but was able to exercise faith about the project. The sense of a shared concern was also very strong among the church members and the willingness to give and to work for this project seemed endless. Hope Home is a catalyst for the compassion of the whole group and a way in which that compassion can reach some very needy children. It would appear to be well named.

4. Task/Question (Group)

What is your response to this story? Are there lessons to be learned about how to approach the suffering of people in troubled areas of the world?

*

Section 5

As well as the issue of these large-scale problem areas of the world, there is the question of our feeling of helplessness in the face of the griefs and pains of our own friends and families. In this area the same principle can apply: offering what we can and trusting God to make the offering effective. The temptation can be to give in to despair and avoid the issue as it makes us feel helpless. If we do not love enough we will not *want* to do anything: if we do not trust enough we will not *be able* to do anything. The activity of prayer itself works in the same way. It is an action *we* do, but it is *God* who makes it effective. This seems to be the way God has chosen to operate with his people: generally, he chooses to change things by involving us in both prayer and action, but we are dependent on him to make both effective.

The question remains for us: why has he chosen to do things this way? There is a deeper question too. Why is so much intervention necessary, if a God in whom there is no darkness made the world in the first place? These are the big questions but we cannot avoid them if we want to exercise unbreakable hope with any kind of integrity. We have to grapple with them at whatever level we can. So let us try to apply the principle of doing what we can and trusting God to make up the shortfall.

Let us consider first of all how a world in which there is so much darkness could have been made by a God in whom there is no darkness at all. We have to conclude that someone — or ones — other than God has been exercising a will contrary to his, and if he made everything and everyone, then one or more than one of his creatures is responsible. This is another area in which the relationship between human parents and children may offer some analogous light on the subject. How far can parents be held responsible for crimes committed by their children? It is after all an issue that those responsible for law and order frequently raise, suggesting compulsory parenting classes, curfews, etc.

There is no doubt that lack of good parenting has contributed hugely to the social problems faced by many deprived areas of our cities, but how do we account for the rarer cases of children who have had every advantage in their upbringing and yet have turned against the values of their parents, and caused havoc wherever they go? What could we expect the feelings of such parents to be when they see their loved and cherished 'creations' perpetrating horrors which they themselves would never countenance? While the child is still under the authority of his or her parents, we could expect severe discipline to be the order of the day, but once the child has reached adulthood, what are the parents to do? If the child has exercised his or her will to bring disgrace upon himself or herself there comes a point at which the parents have no option but to suffer the grief of an estranged child and take whatever steps they can in the way of damage limitation.

5. Task/Question (Group)

Read Isaiah 5:1-7, 'The Song of the Vineyard', for a poetic expression of such parental grief and anger in the heart of God when he considered the behaviour of his chosen people who should have brought blessing to all nations.

*

Section 6

We can understand that for a child to become independent of its parents and become a properly autonomous and responsible adult there has to be the risk that he or she will not uphold the standards taught to him or her in childhood. For God to make a creature that is not simply a clone or a robot, he takes the terrible risk of the self-determining creature going against his light-filled ways. He gives away some of his power into the hands of people who may or may not follow his guidance about how to find true wholeness and realisation. Already we have a world in which darkness can and does prevail in many cases. If God is not to take back his power from his creatures and make them into puppets, he has to allow their wrong decisions, their cruelties, their criminal foolishness and negligence. They have to have the opportunity to see the consequences of their action or — in many cases — their lack of action.

Where the adult children allow their parents to have some influence upon them, the lessons of childhood can be put into practice, but where the adult children close the door to benign parental influence, the parents are restricted to damage limitation and the same is true of God by this analogy. One of the most unbearable aspects of such a situation for human parents must be to see their grandchildren suffering from damaging parenting and not having complete freedom to step in and prevent the damage, but having to try to mop up as best they can. By the time children can be removed from such situations, the damage has usually been done. It is the very fact of having a rogue parent that inflicts the harm on the child. Could it be that a similar agony is to be found in the heart of God when he sees vulnerable ones suffering at the hands of those he has made?

What this amounts to is an acknowledgement that once real power is shared, there will be a price to pay in terms of terrible suffering at worst and unsatisfactoriness at best. Nothing is simple when we are dealing with the human will. The biblical stories of the fall offer explanations of this truth of human experience with which we are all familiar. One of the losses described is the loss of control over the forces of nature which — by implication and sometimes by specific explanation in the text — leaves us at the mercy of earthquakes, storms, wild beasts, unrestricted growth of weeds, plagues, pests and even the pains of our own bodies. The biblical account claims that when the ways of God were disregarded by human beings, they lost their authority over the natural world which was given to them at the beginning and that as a result that natural world became disordered and even dangerous.

By this reasoning, all our troubles arise from a genuine sharing of divine power with human beings — and indeed possibly other created spiritual beings — who cannot or will not wield it correctly and so are leading the amazing and beautiful world into a travesty of its true self. Worse, it is often the innocent who suffer as a result. If this is a true analysis, we still have the question of why God doesn't intervene to put things right with his creation. It is, of course, the Christian contention that he has already done that in the sending of Christ into the world as both the agent and the forerunner of a renewed creation. Therefore, a major part of our investigation into unbreakable hope must surely be to explore this claim, bearing in mind that for many people it is unimpressive, as things still seem to be far from satisfactory two thousand years after Christ's coming. As God did at the beginning of creation, Christ has put things in the hands of fallible human beings, so how has he improved our lot?

6. Task/Question (Group)
Read Mark 4:35-41, the stilling of the storm by Jesus. What does it reveal to the disciples about Jesus?

*

Section 7

It is at this point in our consideration of this matter that the doctrine of the humanity of Christ may come to our aid. Far from being an obscure theological issue, it is central to our question of whether God has intervened in human affairs to set things right. One of Jesus' favourite names for himself was 'The Son of Man', or as we might say it today, 'The Human Being'. Put in this way, it emphasises the idea that he was the only true human being, the only one who fulfilled the potential inherent in everyone, the definitive example of personhood. There was also a certain amount of Messianic expectation associated with the title because of a passage in Daniel chapter 7, verses 13-14, where 'one like a son of man' was given great authority by God. Paul referred to Christ as 'The Last Adam' in 1 Corinthians 15:45-49. These titles suggest that, as well as illustrating what God is, the life of Jesus illustrates what true humanity is. He displays in his earthly life the authority over the natural world which Adam or early man had lost. This gives a significance to Jesus' miracles which is over and above that of expressing compassion to the suffering. He even imparted this authority in some cases to those who believed in him. Peter, for example, was also able to walk on the water for a short time until he took his eyes off Jesus and looked at the wild waves instead.

We know from our own experience that such miraculous powers are not a regular part of our daily lives, and even those whom Jesus healed or raised from the dead, still went on to die in the course of time, as we all do. So what is the importance of these miracles to us as we wonder what difference Jesus' coming has made to the world? In John's gospel, the miracles are referred to as 'signs' and this word is helpful. What are these supernatural events signalling to us? It is probably also significant that there appear to be a number of similarly supernatural occurrences reported when the Christian message is taken to a place which has never heard of it or when there is a reawakening of the Christian faith in a place which used to be Christian but has lapsed.

The miracles are not ends in themselves, although of course they do bring about a resolution of human difficulties as might be expected from an intervention by a merciful God. As Mark records in his account of Jesus stilling the storm, the miracles are meant to make us ask who Jesus is. A danger which Jesus himself recognised was that he would be followed as one who could fulfil all our immediate needs and so prevent, or make unlikely, any further searching into his deeper significance for the human race. He worked this out painfully in his own human experience as he fasted in the desert while preparing for his life's work. He considered making stones into bread to satisfy his physical hunger, but decided that although we need physical food, a deeper human need is to hear God speak. Matthew 4 and Luke 4 give detailed accounts of this struggle.

Another way Jesus might have carried out his mission as the only true human being, was by taking risky actions to 'force' God's hand into a spectacular rescue, but he refused the path of trying to manipulate God or trying to have overall control of when, where and how his vindication would come. On the contrary, at the very moment of his worst agonies, he suffered the mockery of his compatriots who were looking for something spectacular:

> 'He saved others — he can't save himself! King of Israel is he? Then let him get down from that cross. We'll *all* become believers then! He was so sure of God — well, let him rescue his 'Son' now — if he wants him! He did claim to be God's Son didn't he?' (Matthew 27:42-43 *The Message*)

It seems here as in other places that Jesus refused the easy answer: he refused to dazzle people into belief in him. It has never been possible for us to say with any credibility of Jesus, 'Oh it was all very well for him!' as it quite clearly was not all very well for him. He would not take short cuts that left anyone out in the cold but he himself deliberately went out in the cold too. He was convinced that he had to experience the depths of human desolation in order to speak with conviction to all other human beings, whatever their plight. Everything about Jesus' words and actions illustrates the complexity and cost of God's saving intervention in the world, without taking away the need for willing cooperation from the people he wished to save. Magic wands were not an option.

7. Task/Question (Group)

Consider the third way in which Jesus was tempted to carry out his mission in Matthew 4:8-10. What might have been involved in 'bowing down and worshipping Satan', which Jesus refused so categorically to do?

*

Section 8

In this third temptation of Jesus he was shown the kingdoms of the world and their splendour and offered them if he would only direct his worship away from God. The model of earthly splendour about which Jesus would have heard most, would have been the magnificent court of King Solomon, son of David. After the wars David had fought to secure his throne, there was a time of peace during which Solomon amassed wealth and built both the Temple and a great palace in Jerusalem. He also gained a widespread reputation for wisdom and was sought out by the good and the great who wanted to hear his wise sayings, and see his wealthy court.

This took place mid tenth century BC and the account is to be found in the first book of Kings. In chapter 3 is the story of God giving Solomon a 'wish' and Solomon asking for wisdom to govern well. God's reply to this request is found in verses10-14:

> 'God, the Master, was delighted with Solomon's response. And God said to him, 'Because you have asked for this and haven't grasped after a long life, or riches, or the doom of your enemies, but you have asked for the ability to lead and govern well, I'll give you what you've asked for — I'm giving you a wise and mature heart. There's never been one like you before: and there'll be no one after. As a bonus, I'm giving you both the wealth and glory you didn't ask for — there's not a king anywhere who will come up to your mark. And if you stay on course, keeping your eye on the life-map and the God-signs as your father David did, I'll also give you a long life.'(*The Message*)

Thereafter in both the books of Kings and Chronicles the magnificence of this God-given splendour is described and itemised, truly an unimaginable degree of wealth and luxury, wisdom and learning, building projects of massive cost, gardens and pools of legendary beauty. However, Solomon also had a vast harem of wives and concubines, many from various surrounding countries with which Solomon had made treaties and conducted trade on a grand scale. According to the account in Kings, Solomon's wives led him away from the worship of Yahweh and into worshipping other 'gods', whose worship involved degrading practices of various kinds. As a result, most of the kingdom was removed from Solomon's descendants and the greatness of Israel's golden age was dissipated in wars and eventual exile in Babylon.

The Old Testament contains several books attributed to Solomon: many of the Proverbs are pithy distillations of wisdom, the Song of Songs is a famous and beautiful love poem and Ecclesiastes is a reflection on the ultimate futility of life. At this stage in Israel's history, when Solomon ruled, there was no clear belief in life after death and although Solomon saw that wisdom is better than foolishness and that wise behaviour generally improves the quality of life for oneself and others, he also saw that both the wise person and the fool die in the end. Solomon, the man who had everything his heart could desire, said:

> 'Utterly meaningless! Everything is utterly meaningless'
> (Ecclesiastes 1: 2b *NIV*)

8. Task/Question (Group)

Consider question 7 again in the light of this reflection on Solomon. How is a person's view of life affected if he or she misdirects worship to unworthy objects such as money, sex or power?

*

Section 9

As most of us know, the birth of Jesus was the opposite of what we might expect. It took place in an outhouse, there being no place for his parents to stay in comfort as they were poor and displaced by the seemingly arbitrary requirements of the Roman occupying power. In the same way his chosen 'kingship' was the opposite of what we might expect. Jesus had seen the limitations of the way of earthly splendour exemplified by Solomon's court. Even a man of Solomon's wisdom and culture, who appreciated the best this life has to offer, felt the sadness of loss common to us all:

> 'Life, lovely while it lasts, is soon over.
> Life as we know it, precious and beautiful, ends.
> The body is put back in the same ground it came from.
> The spirit returns to God, who first breathed it.'
> (Ecclesiastes 12:6-7 *The Message*)

This statement was in the context of Solomon's encouragement to remember God when we are still young enough to serve him, as old age and death will bring all our efforts to an end. The spirit returning to God meant the end of the individual in Solomon's understanding.

In Matthew's gospel, Jesus mentions Solomon a few times. One of these references occurred when the Jewish leaders were challenging Jesus' authority. This is worth quoting at length because it throws light on several of the relevant issues. These leaders, who were expecting divine intervention in the shape of a 'Messiah' according to their prophets, were sceptical about Jesus.

'A few religion scholars and Pharisees got on him. 'Teacher, we want to see your credentials. Give us some hard evidence that God is in this. How about a miracle?

Jesus said, 'You're looking for proof, but you're looking for the wrong kind. All you want is something to titillate your curiosity, satisfy your lust for miracles. The only proof you're going to get is what looks like the absence of proof: Jonah-evidence. Like Jonah, three days and nights in the fish's belly, the Son of Man will be gone three days and nights in a deep grave.

'On Judgement Day, the Ninevites will stand up and give evidence that will condemn this generation, because when Jonah preached to them they changed their lives. A far greater preacher than Jonah is here, and you squabble about 'proofs'. On Judgement Day, the Queen of Sheba will come forward and bring evidence that will condemn this generation, because she travelled from a far corner of the earth to listen to wise Solomon. Wisdom far greater than Solomon's is right in front of you, and you quibble over 'evidence'.' (Matthew 12:38-42 *The Message*)

Here, Jesus indicates how he is proposing to carry out his saving mission: he is going to face the ultimate enemy of human beings, death itself. What's more, he is going to do so as 'The Son of Man', that is, as a human being. This passage also reveals that there was now, among at least some of the Jews, a clear belief in life after death as those long dead, such as Jonah and the Queen of Sheba, would have a future role to play on what he called 'The Day of Judgement'. Finally, Jesus claims that the wisdom of his going down into death exceeds the wisdom of Solomon, who sought to make sense of this life only. The very idea of a Messiah who would die was nonsense to the Jews.

9. Task/Question:
Read Matthew 16:21-23. As soon as his disciples expressed specifically their belief that he was the expected Messiah, Jesus began telling them how he proposed to fulfil his mission. Try to spell

out the connection between this incident and Jesus' temptations in the desert.

*

Section 10

The confusion about the nature of Jesus' kingship was used by his enemies among the Jewish authorities to blackmail the Roman governor Pontius Pilate into passing the death sentence on Jesus. Pilate was afraid of appearing to be disloyal to Caesar in allowing a Jewish king to hold sway. Some of the few remarks Jesus made at his trials before both the Jewish Council and before Pilate are very revealing. First, before the Jewish Council, in Matthew 26:63-64, when none of the charges against Jesus could be substantiated:

> 'The High Priest said to him, 'I charge you under oath by the living God: Tell us if you are the Christ (Messiah), the Son of God.'
> 'Yes, it is as you say,' Jesus replied. 'But I say to all of you: in the future you will see the Son of Man sitting at the right hand of the Mighty One and coming on the clouds of heaven.'
> (*NIV* brackets mine).

Jesus' acknowledgement that he was the Son of God was enough for the Jews to convict him of blasphemy and they seemed not to hear the point that he was more interested in, that a human being would be sitting at God's right hand in future. Then, in John 18:36, Pilate had been trying to establish whether Jesus was claiming to be a king:

> 'My kingdom is not founded in this world — if it were, my servants would have fought to prevent my being handed over to the Jews. But in fact my kingdom is not founded on all this!
> 'So you are a king, are you?' returned Pilate.
> 'Indeed I am a king,' Jesus replied; 'The reason for my birth and the reason for my coming into the world is to witness to the truth. Every man who loves truth recognises my voice.'
> (J.B. Phillips: *The New Testament in Modern English for Schools*)

The 'wisdom far greater than Solomon's' to which Jesus laid claim, did not seek expression in grandeur, wealth, beauty, learning, power or status as they are commonly understood. Rather than directing his attention merely to the *results* of the estrangement between God and man, which have — in their awful distress and troubles — been *our* usual focus, he majored on the *cause* of the estrangement. According to this last passage, what we need most from his intervention in the world is a recovery of the truth.

The Satanic voice in scriptural accounts always questions the truth of what God has said to his people: ('Did God *really* say....?' in Genesis 3 to the first Adam; '*If* you are the Son of God....' in Matthew 4 to the last Adam. Italics mine.) The sub-text of the Satanic message is always to suggest that God is trying to cheat human beings out of something good — the forbidden fruit, the food necessary for physical survival — while all the time the Satanic purpose is to cheat human beings out of the *restful trust in God's goodness* which is more necessary to our wellbeing than anything else, however desirable or natural. As soon as that trust goes, we feel we are on our own and often try to take things into our own hands with catastrophic results.

The nature of the hope brought by the intervention of Jesus is more radical than any of us is looking for. We would like him to stop a few wars and earthquakes, heal a few incurable illnesses, provide for our physical needs and then go away without requiring anything more. Jesus makes clear that he has an agenda quite different from this. Although he will engage in a certain amount of damage limitation of the kind we think we require, he always presents a challenge to look further and dig deeper than we have been prepared to do. Perhaps we can begin a deeper search as we proceed with our study.

10. Task/Question (Group)
Read Genesis 2:9 and 3:22. Why, according to these verses — and the story in between them if you need to be reminded of it — did death come into human experience? What, in the light of this, could Jesus' purpose have been in deliberately going through death as the only true human being?

Chapter 6: The Lifeline

Section 1

The Jewish creation story in the biblical book of Genesis is a particularly wise attempt to explain the human condition and a detailed study of it yields many life-enhancing insights. For example, I wonder how many of us have been fully aware that in this story of the Garden of Eden, there are *two* significant trees. We all know about the tree of the knowledge of good and evil, the one from which Adam and Eve were forbidden to eat, but do we register the presence of the other significant tree found in the garden? Verse 22 in Genesis 3 draws attention to it in these words:

> 'God said, 'The Man has become like one of us, capable of knowing everything, ranging from good to evil. What if he now should reach out and take fruit from the *Tree-of-Life* and eat, and live for ever? Never — this cannot happen!' (*The Message,* italics mine)

Thereafter, to prevent this, God banishes Adam and Eve from the Garden of Eden, so performing one of his first acts of damage limitation in response to the straying of human beings from his clearly understood guidelines. He sets a limit to the life of human beings on this earth. Understood properly, this is an act of mercy. However painful and unbearable life becomes, it will not go on for ever. (Those who advocate the legalising of euthanasia have grasped this point and, rightly or wrongly, seek to have control of the moment of death as a way to end suffering.) Death can also be seen as a mercy because however cruel or wicked people become, there will be a limit to the time given them to exercise their power to hurt. Seen in this light, death appears as a good thing as it sets a boundary to both suffering and evil in ourselves and in others.

However, we do not usually experience it as a good thing: as Dylan Thomas says in one of his best-loved poems;

> 'Do not go gentle into that good night
> Rage, rage against the dying of the light.'

The wise and the good grieve — or 'rage' as Thomas more powerfully puts it — because they have been able to do so little to improve things. The old grieve at their failing powers, those who are wild grieve because of the harm they have done and it is too late to put things right. Thomas explores these different reasons why we should fight against death, despite calling it 'good'.

There are many reasons to grieve about the fact of our death. We all have a sense of loss, a sense of unrealised potential, a sense of the waste of something infinitely precious, of something god-like spoiled or cut short. Despite its terrors and frustrations, there is a glory about human life of which we all catch glimpses, and we feel that mourning its loss is appropriate.

We also feel a greater or lesser amount of fear at the thought of no longer existing, at least in this present form, and take elaborate precautions to protect our own lives and those of the ones we love from premature or painful death. Human beings are programmed to preserve themselves and will only embrace death in very unusual circumstances and can usually only do so if they exercise exceptional courage. Again, our great poets are able to give expression to this universal fear of death, even when this life seems hard. Shakespeare puts these words into Hamlet's mouth;

'Who would.....
....grunt and sweat under a weary life,
But that the dread of something after death —
The undiscovered country, from whose bourn
No traveller returns — puzzles the will,
And makes us rather bear those ills we have
Than fly to others that we know not of?' (Act 3, Scene 1,)

This passage appears at the end of Hamlet's most famous speech, ('To be or not to be') in which he considers suicide as he is so distraught about the suspected murder of his father by his uncle. The fear of death, 'the undiscovered country', prevents him from taking his own life.

There are, admittedly, some people whose lives have had sufficient happiness, who think this life is enough in itself and say that they are content to die when their time comes. They use phrases such as: 'I've had a good innings' to describe their own contentment. There is something wholesome and realistic about such an approach to death, yet even then, such a statement may express resignation rather than real contentment. Besides, the death of such a person is still accompanied by tears and grief and sometimes the facing of a lonely future by loved ones.

1. Task/Question (By yourself)

Are you able to say what your own attitude to this subject is? Try explaining to a friend or write it down. Have you considered this before? Do you feel in any way prepared for death yourself?

*

Section 2

Let us return to the question of why Jesus decided he could best carry out his mission to bring wholeness by going through death himself. What could death have meant for Jesus, whose presence was always so life-giving to others? His disciples could not accept that it would be anything other than tragic for him to die. Again and again Jesus explained his unimaginable intention to them. Even more unimaginable, he would be raised to life after three days. What he proposed seemed to be a kind of 'going through' death and emerging on the other side. No wonder the disciples were mystified.

The gospel which has most to say about Jesus' purposes in all of this is the gospel of John. Tradition has it that this gospel was written by the disciple John, who was Jesus' best friend or, as he calls himself, 'the disciple whom Jesus loved'. As such, he might be expected to have had most insight into Jesus' inner thoughts and plans. In chapter ten of John's gospel, Jesus uses the image of a shepherd to describe himself. Extracts from verses 14-18 are illuminating:

> 'I am the good shepherd.....and I lay down my life for the sheep.....
> The reason my Father loves me is that I lay down my life — only to take it up again. No-one takes it from me, but I lay it down of my own accord. I have authority to lay it down and authority to take it up again. This command I received from my Father.' (*NIV*)

This passage makes clear that Jesus was convinced he was obeying God by going to Jerusalem so determinedly at that fateful Passover time when he knew opposition to him amongst Jewish religious leaders was at a murderous pitch. Those who should have been leading the way in bringing wholeness to the world, according to their own prophetic writings, failed to recognise in Jesus the one through whom this task could be accomplished. Instead, they regarded him as a threat to their own power base amongst the Jews and decided he should be eliminated.

Jesus showed again and again that he had no illusions about what would happen to him if he challenged them but he also showed that he believed God's mission to bring wholeness would nevertheless be fulfilled. The tradition of a Messiah who would lead his people to victory over their enemies had been seen by many Jews as referring to some sort of military triumph over the occupying power of Rome, but Jesus had drawn on another tradition within Judaism, that of the suffering servant, laying down his life for a straying world.

A famous passage in Isaiah's prophecy chapter 53 describes this servant, who is sometimes seen as the whole of the Jewish race and sometimes only as a faithful core of them or even as one faithful individual. Many of the best-loved parts of Handel's 'Messiah' are taken from this chapter:

> 'He was despised and rejected of men'
> 'Surely he hath borne our griefs and carried our sorrows'
> 'And with his stripes we are healed'
> 'All we like sheep have gone astray...and the Lord hath laid on him the iniquity of us all'.

These are such well known words for some people that their import can easily be lost, so it is helpful to read them in *The Message* version:

> 'He was looked down on and passed over'
> 'But the fact is, it was our pains he carried — our disfigurements, all the things   wrong with us'
> 'Through his bruises we get healed'
> 'We're all like sheep who've wandered off......And God piled all our sins, everything we've done wrong, on him.' (verses 3-6)

Further on in the same chapter, we read these words:

> 'Still, it's what God had in mind all along, to crush him with pain. The plan was that he give himself as an offering for sin so that he'd see life come from it — life, life, and more life. And God's plan will deeply prosper through him. Out of that terrible travail of soul, he'll see that it's worth it and be glad he did it.'
> (Verses 10-11a *The Message*)

2. Task/Question (Group)

An idea which may be useful here is that in Jesus, God the Father has, in a very particular way, 'written himself into the history of the world'. How could this idea help us to understand Jesus' intentions with regard to his mission?

Section 3

The Pauline concept of Jesus being the 'Last Adam' is helpful in that it indicates a contrast between Jesus and the 'First Adam' or early humankind. The first Adam listened to the Satanic voice questioning God's goodness and went on to disobey God because he doubted that goodness. The last Adam, when tempted to doubt God's good purpose, refused to do so and held to what he believed God had said. In terms of the Genesis story of Eden therefore, he then had the right to 'take fruit from the Tree-of-life and eat and live for ever'. So, although he found himself in a world of people banished from Eden, he himself retained his unbroken communication and communion with God and therefore no damage limitation was required in his case. He was free, as he said, to lay down his life and to take it up again at will. He did not 'owe' death anything. He expressed this point in a different way in one of his richly-laden farewell discussions with his disciples:

> 'I'll not be talking with you much more like this because the chief of this godless world is about to attack. But don't worry — he has nothing on me, no claim on me. But so the world might know how thoroughly I love the Father, I am carrying out my Father's instructions right down to the last detail.' (John 14:30-31a *The Message*)

The death of Jesus therefore, by this reasoning, was totally different from the death of anyone else. People sometimes wonder why his death was so particular, as terrible though it was, the Romans crucified many people. Also, many people in the history of the world have died in horrifying, torturous ways. What was so different about his death?

The difference, Christians have always believed, lies in both who Jesus is, and what his purpose in dying was. Any other person who chose to go into circumstances which would almost certainly result in death or terrible torture might be regarded as brave to the point of foolhardiness — such as some of the secret agents during the Second World War — or misguided to the point of madness — such as suicide bombers.

3. Task/Question (Group)
Does Jesus come into either of these categories?

Section 4

Looked at as a whole, the life of Jesus does not suggest madness. On the contrary, he seems to be in control both of himself and the situations that faced him at every point in his ministry. The accounts of his life and death show a man who knew what was coming, wrestled with the agonies of it, took steps to prepare his friends for it, knew why he was doing it and what it would cost, but was quite determined to go ahead with it as he believed it would change the human condition radically in a way that enabled wholeness and life for anyone who wanted it.

We are obviously dealing with a great mystery here and so our explanations will be very partial but what John seems to be saying in his account is that because Jesus did not have to die on his own account, the benefits of his freely offered death could be transferred to others who recognised and loved him and what he was doing, others who wanted a share in his life which could not be kept under the control of death. These others were being offered an opportunity to go through death and out the other side 'on the coat-tails of Jesus' as it were, but only if they were not too proud to accept the offer. The symbolism of baptism reflects this process: the one being baptised goes down under the water to indicate dying with Christ and then comes up out of the water to indicate rising with him into a new life.

In the synoptic gospels — Matthew, Mark and Luke — there appear the famous accounts of the last supper of Jesus and his disciples when Jesus told them that his body would be broken for them and his blood shed for them and for many others, and that they should remember that whenever they ate bread or drank wine together. In the gospel of John, however, that idea is expanded upon in the discussion about the bread of life. This is particularly interesting as it follows on in John chapter 6 from the account of the feeding of the five thousand, the incident we considered earlier, in which Jesus performed a sign which pointed to who he was. The crowd who had been fed miraculously chased after Jesus and he said to them:

> 'Don't waste your energy striving for perishable food like that. Work for the food that sticks with you, food that nourishes your lasting life, food the Son of Man provides...... I am the Bread of Life. The person who aligns with me hungers no more and thirsts no more, ever. I have told you this explicitly because even though

you have seen me in action, you don't really believe me.....I have come down from heaven not to follow my own whim but to accomplish the will of the One who sent me.

This, in a nutshell, is that will: that everything handed over to me by my Father be completed — not a single detail missed — and at the wrap-up of time I have everyone and everything put together, upright and whole. This is what my Father wants: that anyone who sees the Son and trusts who he is and what he does and then aligns with him will enter *real* life, *eternal* life. My part is to put them on their feet alive and whole at the completion of time....The Bread that I present to the world so that it can eat and live is myself, this flesh-and-blood self.'

(Verses 26-27a, 35-36, 38-40 and 51b *The Message*)

These are quite amazing claims, and if true, they put Jesus in a category of his own in the history of the world. Here, he takes onto his own shoulders the task given to the whole Jewish race at the time of Abraham, and now to Jesus as representative of the true Israel — that of restoring the wholeness of the world and the human race. By the imagery of Eden, the cross becomes the 'Tree-of-Life' and the fruit of the tree that gives real eternal life to people, is the body and blood of Jesus, offered not on his own account, but on the account of anyone who wants it. The cost of allowing human beings back into Eden — or into restored harmony with God — is inescapable when we look at the crucifixion of Jesus.

At the time when these words about the bread of life were first spoken, John records that there was quite a reaction against them. Many of Jesus' followers turned away from him thinking he was saying something grotesque because they were thinking literally about consuming his body and blood. Jesus asked the disciples if they wanted to leave him too, and Peter spoke for them:

'Master, to whom would we go? You have the words of real life, eternal life. We've already committed ourselves, confident that you are the Holy One of God.' (John 6:68-69 *The Message*)

There was recognition amongst those who knew him best that his words were not empty boasting. They may not have understood or accepted his way of tackling the task of bringing wholeness to the world, but they felt he was 'the real thing' and had the authority to tackle it.

An interesting aspect of these claims by Jesus is his repeated reference to 'the end of time' or 'the last day' in some translations. He suggests his task will not be completed until the end of time. This has various significant implications: for example, the work of bringing wholeness is one that takes time and cannot be rushed. It takes as long as it takes, although there are undoubtedly moments when the process seems to take a great stride forward.

Another implication of Jesus' reference to the end of time, of course, is that he himself will be there, despite his plan to face death at the hands of the Romans by the agency of the Jewish religious authorities. At this point therefore, it is appropriate to look at the resurrection of Jesus and to ask what kind of resurrection it was.

4. Task/Question (Group)

Can you imagine anything good coming out of the fact that most of the Jews — and certainly most of the religious leaders — did not accept that Jesus was the promised Messiah they had been waiting for? Consult Romans chapters 9-11 for a Pauline interpretation of this question.

*

Section 5

A clue about Jesus' own interpretation of his death comes in John's gospel, chapter 12, verse 24. He had been approached by some Gentiles — Greeks — who wanted to see him and he replied by saying:

> 'I tell you the truth, unless a grain of wheat falls to the ground and dies, it remains only a single seed. But if it dies, it produces many seeds.'

It seems he felt that his death would break open the possibility of wholeness to more than simply the Jewish nation, whereas during his life he had always focussed on that nation alone and encounters with Gentiles were unusual — although very significant when they did occur. On this occasion, Jesus seemed to indicate that the time for Greeks and other Gentiles to 'meet' him would come later, after his death and resurrection had secured the promise of wholeness he was coming to bring.

The offer to the Jews was to come first and be rejected by the majority of them. In the history of the growing church, persecution of the Christian Jews by the other Jews was one of the engines which drove many of them into the surrounding nations with the message of wholeness in Jesus Christ. Most significantly, it was the death of

Stephen, at the hands of the Jewish religious authorities because of his Christian faith, which affected the fanatical persecutor of the church, Saul, and played a part in his conversion into Paul, the Apostle to the Gentiles.

The resurrection appearances of Jesus seem to have been a much more private affair than his ministry and death, which were widely known about — the crucifixion of course, was a public spectacle. After his death, however, perhaps surprisingly, Jesus did not appear publicly to show that he had overcome death or that he had got the better of the Jewish religious authorities. The only people who saw him were his followers. Paul lists them partially in 1 Corinthians 15:6-8. Others are mentioned at the end of the gospels. Luke gives most details at the end of his gospel and at the beginning of his sequel, the Acts of the Apostles.

Taking all these accounts together, what seems to have happened, according to the biblical narratives, is that Jesus appeared from time to time to his followers for a period of a few weeks after his death, and then, instead of dying again naturally, he was taken away out of their sight in what the church has come to call 'The Ascension', at which time a promise was given that he would return in the same way at some unspecified time in the future.

The question of who would see Jesus after his resurrection crops up in the farewell speeches Jesus gave to his disciples as recorded in John's gospel. In chapter 14, verses 19 and 21, Jesus says:

> 'In just a little while, the world will no longer see me, but you're going to see me because I am alive and you're about to come alive.......The person who knows my commands and keeps them, that's who loves me. And the person who loves me will be loved by my Father, and I will love him and make myself plain to him.' (*The Message*)

One of the disciples then questioned Jesus about the reason for this, and he repeated the point that only those who love him would see him.

Jesus' rising from the dead therefore was essentially different from that of Lazarus, whom Jesus had raised from death during his ministry. Lazarus, as well as any others who were raised from death, went on to die in the natural way as we all do, their span of life simply having been extended for a while, and they were seen by everyone in the usual way. Jesus' resurrection appearances on the contrary were anything but ordinary. For one thing, he was often not recognised at first. The two disciples on the road to Emmaus, for example, only recognised him after he had been speaking with them for some time, explaining how the death of the Messiah was to be expected if the Old Testament prophecies were properly understood. Mary Magdalene thought he was the gardener at first, and when Jesus appeared to a group of the disciples on the shores of the Sea of Galilee, he was not recognised immediately. Significantly it was John who first realised it was Jesus. In John 21:7 we read:

> 'Then the disciple Jesus loved said to Peter, 'It's the Master!'
> (*The Message*)

5. Task/Question (Group)

What could be the reason for the fact that only those who loved him were shown Jesus in his resurrection body? Wouldn't it have been better for him to show himself to the world and convince every one of who he was and what he had done? Think about the original reason for the banishment from Eden and what might be needed for readmittance. Read Revelation 2: 1-7, the message to one of the early churches in Asia.

*

Section 6

It seems that the time for Jesus to challenge the opposition was *before* his death, but that after his resurrection, there would be no bludgeoning of unbelievers with the truth they did not want to hear. Jesus was not into point scoring, and the resurrection life was only for those who loved him and wanted what he had to offer. Human beings were not to be deprived of their power to choose their own path. A person who disliked Christ would not be capable of the life he offered. The seventeenth century poet Samuel Butler composed a couplet which sums up this point well:

> 'He that complies against his will;
> Is of his own opinion still.' (*Hudibras*, part 3.)
> or in Jesus' phrase:
> 'He who has ears, let him hear.' (E.g. in Matthew 13:9 *NIV*)

There is, therefore, an element of the 'open secret' about the resurrection life of Christ. People were not to be bribed with a promise of eternal life. Rather, they were to be shown Jesus to see if they were ready to respond to him. A life of wholeness does not always appeal to a broken person, who may prefer the familiar, dysfunctional life he or she knows. The freedom and responsibility of the life offered may seem too scary. The emphasis of the Christian message is first on *quality* of life, and only then, on *quantity.*

Of course, despite all the warnings Jesus had given them, it was so astonishing for the disciples to see Jesus after his death that they had great difficulty in believing it was him. The story of doubting Thomas bears witness to this in John 20:24-29. Jesus took the problem seriously and made sure they knew it was really him.

> 'Jesus appeared to them and said, 'Peace be with you.' They thought they were seeing a ghost and were scared half to death. He continued with them, 'Don't be upset, and don't let all these doubting questions take over. Look at my hands: look at my feet — it's really me. Touch me. Look me over from head to toe. A ghost doesn't have muscle and bone like this.' As he said this, he showed them his hands and his feet. They still couldn't believe what they were seeing. It was too much: it seemed too good to be true. He asked, 'Do you have any food here?' They gave him a piece of leftover fish they had cooked. He took it and ate it right before their eyes.' (Luke 24:36b -43 *The Message*)

He was also able to appear to them even when they had locked the doors, so although he had a genuine flesh and blood body, which he was at pains to point out, that body did not appear to be subject to the restrictions that ours are. His resurrection body was obviously of a different order.

As usual, we find the implications of all this worked out in Paul's writings: for example in 1 Corinthians 15. The whole chapter is valuable in this matter, but let us look at a few verses in particular. He was challenging the assertion some were making that there was no hope of life after death and saying that if that were the case, then all he and the other apostles had been doing would have been a waste of time. He then continued:

> 'But the glorious fact is that Christ *did* rise from the dead: he has become the very first to rise of all who sleep the sleep of death.....
> As members of a sinful race all men die; as members of the Christ of God all men shall be raised to life, each in his proper order, with Christ the very first and after him all who belong to him when he

comes...The last enemy of all to be destroyed is death itself.....
The body is 'sown' in corruption: it is raised beyond the reach of
corruption. It is 'sown' in dishonour: it is raised in splendour. It
is 'sown' in weakness: it is raised in power. It is 'sown' a natural
body: it is raised a spiritual body.'
(Verses 20, 22 -23, 26,42b -44a *The New Testament in Modern
English for Schools* translated by J.B. Phillips.)

Here Paul attempts to describe the indescribable: the nature of
Christ's resurrection body, which Paul claims is the prototype of the
resurrection bodies of all who trust themselves to him.

6. Task/Question (Group)
Read again John 6:4a in *The Message* translation: 'This is what my
Father wants: that anyone who sees the Son and trusts who he is and
what he does and then aligns with him will enter *real* life, *eternal* life.'
Can you see a connection between these words and the *'restful trust
in God's goodness'* which Jesus held onto when he was being tempted
(as we considered in the tenth section of chapter 5)?

*

Section 7

In Jesus, are we being shown what being human really means? Are
we seeing a life lived in complete harmony with God, whom Jesus
describes as his 'Father'? Do we see someone who was unreservedly
committed to doing what he believed his Father wanted, no matter
what it cost him? Perhaps we are being shown what might have
happened if the first Adam had chosen to pick the fruit from the tree
of life instead of from the tree of the knowledge of good and evil.

Yet even if the earliest human beings *had* made such a choice,
they would have been in a state of innocence, never having strayed;
whereas those who embrace Christ *do* know good and evil and
are seeking to be restored. Perhaps this puts them in a stronger
position as they are actively choosing life having known the 'death' of
disharmony with God. There is even a church tradition which finds
expression in the Missal, claiming that Adam's sin was a good thing
because it resulted in such redemption as Christ offers:

'O felix culpa, quae talem ac tantum meruit habere Redemptorem.'
'O happy fault, which has deserved to have such and so mighty a
Redeemer.'('Exsultet' on Holy Saturday.)

This obviously twists the commonly understood meaning of the word, 'happy', yet its force is clear. To use a musical metaphor, a discord resolved is often more satisfying to the ear than unbroken concord. Jesus himself, by this analysis, would be in the strongest position of all, being an innocent in his own life and conduct, but knowing evil and death by submitting himself willingly to them in order to open a way forward for those who would otherwise be subject to death on their own account.

At this point, we may have questions about a God who seemed to require such a sacrifice as Jesus made when he claimed especially to have blessed Jesus with his favour. Lest we begin to think of God as being very hard on Jesus, we need to call on another central doctrine of Christianity: that of the divinity of Christ. Again, far from being an obscure theological issue, this doctrine is a vital plank in the bridge which supports the unbreakable hope we are examining, the hope that spans the gulf between life as it is and life as it should and can be. And again, John's gospel is very illuminating. It begins with a famous passage which deliberately echoes the opening of Genesis ('In the beginning God created the heavens and the earth.') John's opening reads:

> 'In the beginning was the Word, and the Word was with God, and the Word was God. Through him all things were made; without him nothing was made that has been made. In him was life, and that life was the light of men. The light shines in the darkness, but the darkness has not understood it........He was in the world, and though the world was made through him, the world did not recognise him..... The Word became flesh and made his dwelling among us. We have seen his glory, the glory of the One and Only, who came from the Father, full of grace and truth.'
> (Verses 1 -3, 10 and 14 *NIV*)

Thereafter, John the gospel writer goes on to say how John the Baptist drew attention to this 'true light' and identified the light as Jesus himself. From the earliest days of Christianity therefore, amongst those who had lived with Jesus, there was a belief that he was not only a man, but God himself, having become a part of his own creation, carrying out the action required if human beings were not to be irretrievably lost to him, paying the price — foreseen from the beginning — of sharing his divine power with those who would abuse it.

7. Task/Question (Group)

What could possibly be the reason for such an undertaking on the part of God? Can we look into these mysteries without losing ourselves in things that are too deep for us? Consult Genesis 1: 26 — 27, 31a; Genesis 3:9; Genesis 6:5 — 6; and perhaps the most famous verse in the Bible, John 3:16.

*

Section 8

In the light of all of these considerations, can we say that what Christians see as the intervention of God in human affairs, in the person of Jesus, has made it possible for us to exercise unbreakable hope? How, in practical terms, does this impinge on our view of life in this world and our own lives in particular?

Imagine the life of a Christian believer as the baton in the last part of a relay race, involving the last two runners in the winning team. We could think of his or her natural life as being the second last runner in the team who is becoming weary — he knows he will have to stop soon. Before he does, however, the final runner in the team — whom we could see as Christ himself — runs alongside him for a little while and during that time, the baton is passed to the final runner who speeds away to the finishing line and a successful conclusion to the race. The second last runner then drops out of the race, exhausted, but he is content to stop because he sees his running mate is taking the team to victory.

It is not an exact analogy of course, but it may help us to see the death of a Christian believer as not ultimate, if the most important part of his or her life has been transferred to Christ during this life and will be carried forward by him into the next when the believer's natural life comes to an end. Also, during the time when the two runners are running side by side — the period of the life of a Christian in this world by the analogy we are considering — the energy of the last runner, who is fresh, communicates itself to the tiring runner, and enables him to let go with a peaceful mind, trusting the baton to the stronger runner. Paul says something very like this to his adopted son Timothy in his second letter to Timothy, chapter 1, verse 12:

> 'I know whom I have believed, and am convinced that he is able to guard what I have entrusted to him for that day.' (*NIV*)

This thought enabled Paul to endure the suffering he was going through at the time of writing as he felt that his life and work for good would not be in vain because it was in Christ's care. The fact that so many all over the world today are continuing to draw wisdom and strength from Paul's writing, suggests that it was a sound belief.

Before the Ascension, Jesus took care to point out that, whether his followers could see him or not, he would always be with them and they were to make sure that the offer of wholeness in him was made known to as many people as possible throughout the whole world. Baptism in his name was to be the way for people to embrace Christ and teaching Christ's ways was to be the business of his followers.

As usual, the practical implications of all this are spelled out by Paul — as well as others — in his various letters which are contained in the New Testament. Much of his teaching draws on the concept that the un-Christ-like tendencies of Christians will die anyway — in fact, are already dead in one sense — so why spend time or attention on them? The parts of Christians that are eternal deserve their best attention, as time and energy spent on them will never be lost or wasted.

8. Task/Question (Group)

Consult such a passage by Paul, for example Colossians 3:1-14 (It is particularly vivid in *The Message* translation). Try to say how it might help Christian believers to think of some of their characteristics as dead — or at least doomed — and others as eternal.

*

Section 9

The purposes of Jesus and of his Father, then, according to the Christian message, centre on the restoration of the broken harmony between God and his creation. All the ills of the world which seem to militate against hope, by this interpretation are merely symptoms of that broken harmony. If this is true, we need so much more than simply the removal of distress, trouble and pain. We need the strong, loving, trustful bond with the Creator himself, in order to live freely and creatively in the world.

Such a relationship may well seem beyond the reach of people whose only experience of life has been in such a broken world as ours. Truly a new humanity is required to be equal to such lofty company, a race of heroes and giants surely? Yet those who first entered the new life seemed very ordinary men and women, subject to the failures, weaknesses and inadequacies that plague us all. The very fact that we in the third millennium are studying the person who started it all is testimony to the enduring power of the life, death and resurrection of Jesus, even when conveyed to us through such ordinary people.

The strength to live well in this life and to have an unbreakable hope for both this life and the next seems to have been granted to millions of Christ's followers, simply by means of their trusting in him. He is the one who is equal to the relationship with God the Father, and we have the option to 'get in on his ticket' so to speak, and then begin learning the life skills we need for the new life, taking up our new status as adopted sons and daughters of God himself.

Of course, all this needs to be studied, experienced, learned, 'unpacked' and practised in real situations if it is to mean anything at all, and in many ways, it is a lifetime's task, in which millions of people the world over are engaged. Perhaps it may be valuable at this point, to examine the experience of one person who has accepted the new life available in Christ, to see whether unbreakable hope is really made possible by the intervention of God into the world in the person of Jesus.

A Personal Experience of Christ

As it is of course the case I know best, I will describe as best I can my own experience of becoming a follower of Christ, attempting to convey the ways in which it has enabled me to exercise real hope in the face of the darker aspects of life as we all experience them. Before doing so, however, I should like to emphasise that this is only one person's experience, and that there are as many ways of coming to the same hopeful position in Christ as there are people to do so. I have heard many variations on this theme, depending on each person's background, circumstances, experiences and personality.

Looked at from a certain point of view, my life has been one of privilege and plenty: born in a comparatively wealthy part of the world, in Edinburgh in Scotland, to white, middle class parents, I have not known the extremes of deprivation which are the lot of many people in the world. There was a certain post-Second World War austerity in my childhood, but my father was never unemployed and he worked as a church minister with a regular stipend — not so much that my parents did not have to practise economies, but enough — and a big, rather chilly, old manse as a tied house.

Both my parents had a university education, but it was the time when wives would give up their careers after marriage and devote themselves to their husbands and children. Accordingly, my mother brought her considerable abilities to the care and upbringing of her four children of whom I was the eldest. We lived, happily, in a village in Berwickshire until I was seven and thereafter my father went to minister in a big city church in Nairobi, Kenya, so we all lived there for the next nine years, also happily still in privileged circumstances, but not far from obvious and extreme poverty.

9. Task/Question (By yourself)

What part might a person's background play in determining the amount of hope he or she is able to exercise in adult life? Look at the background of one or two people you know well — maybe even your own — and try to see if there is or is not any correlation between the person's background and his or her level of genuine hope for the world or him or herself.

*

Section 10

I expect you came to the conclusion that there are more variables than simply a person's background which may influence his or her ability to exercise real hope, as opposed to merely optimism. In any case, the advantages and disadvantages I experienced were much as you might expect for a daughter of the manse, which were, on the one hand: a thorough grounding in Christian teaching, practice and example; a loving home and family; a good education; contact with people of very different kinds on a regular basis, and on the other: a high expectation of responsible behaviour from a very young age; living life in a bit of a goldfish bowl; a requirement to perform and take a lead before I was really ready to do so.

The combined effect of these elements was to produce a teenager who was well informed about the Christian life and well trained in its practice but lacking in the self-knowledge that comes from experience of life and finding it difficult to relate to the popular culture of her peers in the turbulent sixties — although in Kenya we were distanced to a certain extent from its effects.

Nevertheless, I had a happy childhood, and experiences of other cultures which few Scottish girls of my age had. I responded positively to the picture of Christ given to me by my parents and developed a childlike faith in him, which was expressed in prayer, worship, study and moral effort — all at a level appropriate to my young age. At the time when other children were growing out of their Sunday school versions of Jesus and drifting away from Christian circles, I was forging a more mature understanding of him. The moment when I felt I was praying to an empty room became, for example, under my mother's guidance, the moment when I stopped relying on feelings alone to be aware of God's presence.

As we belonged to a denomination which practised infant baptism, I had been baptised before I was aware of it, and so the critical moment for me was the time of confirmation of baptism. At the age of fifteen, a year before sitting O-level exams, I decided I would join the confirmation class which my father was leading, so that I could give it my attention before academic pressures built up too much. My father therefore, was the one who helped me to recognise, in the awakened interest I felt in the person of Jesus, the call to be a disciple in my own right.

The service of confirmation went ahead as planned, and a number of other young people and I were confirmed and admitted to full church membership. During the service about three of the church elders came forward to give us 'the right hand of fellowship' and to welcome us on behalf of the whole congregation. For me, that was a very significant moment. Although I was sure that being confirmed was what I wanted to do, I had not expected any special revelation at the time, but as it turned out, I was given an overwhelming and moving sense of the truth that Jesus' death was for me *in particular*, as well as for human beings in general. It was a defining moment indeed. I felt I had been admitted to a very fortunate company, and I was filled with gratitude and wonder. I too was to be included in the life offered. I had a sense of the grace of God, which generously surrounded me, even me.

10. Task/Question (By yourself)

Think of an experience of your own which brought that same sense to you — that you were fortunate to be included in some benefit or some group of people. Try to give a written or spoken account of that moment of grace. It could be the experience of falling in love, for example, when suddenly 'ordinary' love songs acquired a heightened significance and you realised that you were not the only one to have felt like that, but that millions of people the world over could testify to the validity of your experience.

Chapter 7: The Friend

Section 1

And then I lived happily ever after? Quite the reverse — in fact it would not be exaggerating to say that the next six or seven years were the hardest of my fifty-nine-year-old life so far. Of course many of the struggles I faced were common to all teenagers making the transition to independent, adult life, but there was an additional strain I experienced precisely because of having embarked on a life of Christian discipleship at the age of fifteen.

In a nutshell, I was discovering how unable I was to fulfil what I understood to be the requirements of a truly Christian life. Not only was I daunted by the imperative to do something about the dire need I saw around me in the streets of Nairobi, but I couldn't even master my own selfish tendencies in relation to my immediate family. I was consumed with nervousness when asked to participate vocally in services of worship, and felt unable to share the Christian message with my school friends. In short, I was constantly aware of demands to which I felt quite unequal.

These issues were compounded by the fact that I was embarking on the most intensive stage of my academic life, and also by the fact that my family returned to Scotland at that point. I finished my schooling therefore, in an unfamiliar setting in Aberdeen, although I basically enjoyed being both a school pupil and then a student at Durham University. It was while I was at Durham that I came across people who were involved in what came to be known as the 'Charismatic Movement'.

Unfortunately, since then, this movement has come to have a bad name in many Christian circles because of various excesses and wrong turnings and it has petered out as a distinct movement without apparently realising to any great degree the potential it seemed to have at the beginning in the late sixties (See also Section 5 of this chapter). Nevertheless, contact with it has revolutionised my experience of the Christian faith — and, I believe, that of many others — so my conviction is that it is a key part of the unbreakable hope we are examining.

At this point, we need to turn to another central doctrine of the faith — the doctrine of the Holy Spirit. For this purpose, we must return to the last days of Jesus' life before the crucifixion, and to his resurrection appearances, which were the occasions on which he spoke most specifically about the Holy Spirit. John's account of the farewell discourses between Jesus and his disciples contain — as we might expect — some useful material:

> 'I will talk to the Father, and he'll provide you another Friend so that you will always have someone with you. This Friend is the Spirit of Truth. The godless world can't take him in because it doesn't have eyes to see him, doesn't know what to look for. But you know him already because he has been staying with you, and will even be *in* you!'
> 'When the Friend I plan to send you from the Father comes — the Spirit of Truth issuing from the Father — he will confirm everything about me. You, too, from your side must give your confirming evidence, since you are in this with me from the start.'
> 'I still have many things to tell you, but you can't handle them now. But when the Friend comes, the Spirit of Truth, he will take you by the hand and guide you into all the truth there is. He won't draw attention to himself, but will make sense out of what is about to happen and, indeed, out of all that I have done and said. He will honour me; he will take from me and deliver it to you.' (John 14: 16 -17 and John 15: 26 — 27 and John 16: 12 — 14 *The Message*)

1. Task/Question (Group)

Have you had any awareness of the Holy Spirit and his function? Can you appreciate the point that Christians might need supernatural help to understand and embrace the person of Christ and his work in the world?

*

Section 2

At the end of chapter 5, we looked at a passage earlier in John's gospel in which Jesus told Pilate that the main reason for his own life was to witness to *the truth*, and here, he tells his disciples to expect the Spirit of Truth to come to them after he himself is no longer with them in the flesh. The Spirit of Truth therefore is the same as the Spirit of Christ himself, but instead of being confined to his own person, it is to fill all his disciples, constantly making the life of Christ real and intelligible to them and constantly imparting Christ's life to them.

Luke speaks of this same Spirit as *the power* of Christ. At Jesus' last resurrection appearance, he was telling the disciples to spread the message of wholeness and forgiveness in his name and he finished with the following words:

> 'You're the witnesses. What comes next is very important: I am sending what my Father promised to you, so stay here in the city until he arrives, until you're equipped with power from on high.' (Luke 24: 48 — 49 *The Message*)

Luke then takes up the same point in his second book, the Acts of the Apostles.

> 'You will receive power when the Holy Spirit comes on you; and you will be my witnesses in Jerusalem, and in all Judea and Samaria, and to the ends of the earth.' (Acts 1: 8 *NIV*)

The essential point here is that no follower of Christ is expected to be able to live the new life alone. It is not a relentless and ultimately futile moral effort to make ourselves into mini-Christs by sheer will power. Rather it is the receiving of the actual life of Christ and allowing it to bear fruit in the character and personality of each individual, as well as in the Christian community as a whole, allowing the old ways to fade and wither through lack of use. It is the restoring of the restful trust in God's goodness which has been lost.

The occasion of the coming of the Holy Spirit to the first followers of Christ is recorded in Acts chapter 2 and occurred on the Jewish festival of Pentecost or harvest home, seven weeks after the resurrection of Christ and ten days after his ascension. As soon as the early disciples had had the chance to understand that Jesus was not dead, he withdrew his visible presence from them, so that he could come to them in the form of the Holy Spirit.

Another useful reference to this event is made earlier in John's gospel chapter 7, verses 37-39. Jesus was preaching at the temple in Jerusalem during the Feast of Tabernacles, when the Jews remembered the time of their wandering in the desert before settling in the promised land of Israel:

> 'On the final and climactic day of the Feast, Jesus took his stand. He cried out, 'If anyone thirsts, let him come to me and drink. Rivers of living water will brim and spill out of the depths of anyone who believes in me this way, just as the Scripture says.'

(He said this in regard to the Spirit, whom those who believed in him were about to receive. The Spirit had not yet been given because Jesus had not yet been glorified.)' (*The Message*)

The gospel writer here refers to the process of Jesus 'being glorified' as a prerequisite for the coming of the Holy Spirit to his followers, and further on in John's account, in chapter 17, verses 4-5, we read some words of Jesus on the same subject in one of his last prayers on earth. He speaks to his Father:

'I glorified you on earth by completing down to the last detail what you assigned me to do. And now, Father, glorify me with your very own splendour, the very splendour I had in your presence before there was a world.' (*The Message*)

This prayer of Jesus shows that his 'being glorified' means his being returned to a position of honour at God's side after having finished his terrible task on earth.

2. Task/Question (Group)
Is Jesus suffering from delusions of grandeur in this prayer to his Father? In considering your answer, consult John 17: 1-3, which appear just before the quoted extract, and think about the reason for Jesus' desire to be at God's side again.

*

Section 3

Far from being something which fed Jesus' own vanity, this was an essential part of the restoration of humankind to harmony with their Creator, because even though on the cross, Jesus had been cursed with all the ills of the world, his own integrity and compassion were such that this burden did not extinguish his life permanently. He had the power and the right to take his own humanity and that of his followers right into the presence of God, having broken through the barrier of death itself.

This was the point at which the Spirit of God could be poured out upon human beings, because the actions of Jesus had opened the sluice gate of God's grace. Jesus was a person who had the unreserved endorsement of God, a person who, at huge cost and in obedience to God, brought about restored wholeness for anyone who wanted it. When he addressed the crowds at the Feast of Tabernacles, Jesus used the imagery of water to illustrate the operation of the Holy Spirit in people. Each person so filled would become a source of life him or herself, 'overflowing' onto those around with the life he or she had been given by Christ.

On the day of Pentecost, the form taken by the Spirit was that of a strong wind and fire, symbols of power and purifying energy, and the effect on the disciples was that they found themselves describing God's wonderful actions in languages they had not learned, but which were understood by the Jews of many nations who had gathered to celebrate the feast of Pentecost.

It was the ideal time and place for the message about Christ to be broadcast, and unschooled Peter, the one who had denied knowing Christ only a few weeks before, then spoke in his own tongue with powerful confidence and conviction about what Christ had done and how people could benefit from it. There is no need to say more, as we know that the church expanded hugely in response to this message and survived the often severe persecution of its early days, Paul's mission to the Gentiles complementing that of Peter to the Jews. The rest — as they say — is history.

In the letters of the New Testament, there are various lists of both the fruit of the Holy Spirit — as in Galatians 5:22: where love, joy, peace, patience, kindness, goodness, faithfulness, gentleness and self-control are mentioned — and the gifts of the Spirit — as in Romans 12: 6-8, where preaching, serving, teaching, encouraging, giving and leadership are mentioned or as in 1 Corinthians 12:8-10, where the word of wisdom, the word of knowledge, faith, healing, miracles, prophesy, distinguishing between spirits, speaking in tongues and interpreting tongues are mentioned.

3. Task/Question (By yourself)

Go through these lists of spiritual fruit and gifts in the order that they appear above. Notice the degree of comfort — or otherwise — you experience as you progress through the list. Try to give a reason for your feelings about the fruit and gifts.

*

Section 4

Typical western Christians will usually have no problem in recognising the value of the fruit of the Spirit, even if they feel the lack of them in their lives. They may reckon that if they try a bit harder, they will be able to demonstrate some of these qualities. Then the first list of gifts sounds reasonable too. After all, all these activities are required in the life of any church — or even in any other organisation — in some form or another. In fact, most church members of long standing will find themselves involved in exercising one or other of the gifts in the first list. So far, so good. But what about that troubling second list of gifts?

Understanding what they are is the first point of difficulty: for example, what is the difference between faith as a spiritual gift as listed here and the faith all Christians exercise when they decide to follow Christ? The answer to that question may be found in considering the other area of difficulty many people experience with this second list: the clearly miraculous element in most of them. The gift that has caused the most controversy is — ironically — the one Paul describes as a lesser gift in 1 Corinthians 14: speaking in tongues.

Because the first giving of God's Spirit on the day of Pentecost was accompanied by this phenomenon, some Christians have insisted that all Christians must speak in tongues as evidence that they have received the Holy Spirit. Something which happened spontaneously on that occasion, and on many others since, has been made into a law with which to condemn or devalue the faith of other Christians. This is obviously a travesty of the loving Spirit of Christ and it has caused much unnecessary distress.

Nevertheless, there is, in this list of miraculous gifts, a good corrective to our western ways of thinking which demand rational explanations and proofs before acknowledging the value of anything. Not only that, but it is quite possible to rationalise away the essential part played by the Holy Spirit if we confine ourselves to the lists of fruit and the gifts that seem to be related to a person's natural character and talents. However, when it comes to miracles, our helplessness is thrown into sharp focus. How can we perform a physical miracle simply by being a loving person, for example? How could we heal someone instantly simply by being a good preacher? There is obviously an aspect of the ministry of Jesus and his first disciples which went into realms most of us have not experienced very often, if at all.

This aspect of the Charismatic Movement has caused endless difficulties for many people who have felt that their faith must be lacking if they have prayed for healings that have not happened, for example. People who were ill have had the added burden of feeling that it was their own fault because they did not believe sufficiently. Well documented healings have occurred certainly, but not always and not to order. The Spirit of God is not in anyone's pocket or under anyone's control and there is a scary moment for any person who launches out into the area of the miraculous when his or her total dependence must be on God.

Because this is such a frightening area for most people in our western world, and because there can be serious harm done to others if this is not handled sensitively, many Christians will not have anything to do with the more obviously miraculous end of the spectrum of spiritual gifts, and they have sometimes been left to the lunatic fringe of the church or to cranks and charlatans.

4. Task/Question (By yourself)

Consider your own experiences of the miraculous — or ones you have heard about — and try to assess their snags and/or benefits with the benefit of hindsight.

*

Section 5

But what *is* the significance of the Holy Spirit for today's disciples?

During the course of the twentieth century, there has been something of a rediscovery of the gifts of the Holy Spirit. In the early years of the century the Pentecostal denominations were formed. As has so often been the case when a neglected aspect of the faith has been rediscovered, those involved at first had no idea of forming a new denomination, but because of opposition in existing denominations, felt — rightly or wrongly — that they had no alternative in the end.

Denominations such as the Methodist Pentecostal Church and the Assemblies of God have attracted huge followings of people in Chile and Brazil although the Pentecostal movement as a whole began in the States and spread to Europe first. There has also been an explosive growth of indigenous Pentecostal churches in Chile, Brazil and South Africa at a time when the historic Protestant denominations were in decline. Something powerful has obviously been happening.

The Charismatic Movement of the sixties and seventies represented another development. Within the historic denominations themselves, both Protestant and Catholic, there was a rediscovery and exercise of spiritual gifts which appeared to happen spontaneously in various places in the world at once. Organisations such as the Fountain Trust in the UK were set up to help promote 'Renewal' as it came to be called. The organisers — showing unusual humility — disbanded the trust when it seemed that its task — to re-emphasise the role of the Holy Spirit within the existing churches — was done.

However, the charismatic gifts of the more miraculous variety, were not, in many cases, integrated properly into the historic denominations, and in many churches, there were explosive breakdowns in communication leading some church members to feel that they had been trying to pour 'new wine into old wineskins', something Jesus warned against in all the synoptic gospels, for example in Mark 2:22:

> 'No-one pours new wine into old wineskins. If he does, the wine will burst the skins, and both the wine and the wineskins will be ruined. No, he pours new wine into new wineskins.' (*NIV*)

In context, Jesus was referring to the fact that his new message could not be forced into an old legalistic system, but it needed new means of expression. Something like this destructive bursting has taken place in many churches and — as so often in church history before — new denominations were formed in which it was hoped the rediscovered aspects of the faith could find freedom of expression.

At first, the House Church Movement seemed to offer a context in which this might happen and there was a time of bright expectation during which some promising new forms of church life seemed to be taking shape. However, the new-found freedom came under attack almost at once: many people in the new churches could not hold onto the freedom they had, and instead of expecting to be shown the appropriate expression of the faith in their own situation by the leading of the Spirit, they looked sideways to apparently successful churches in other places. They drafted in 'experts' from these churches to tell them how to do it or they submitted themselves to charismatic leaders, many of whom, unfortunately, were 'empire-building' on their own account.

Others tied themselves up with expensive and arguably unnecessary building projects. In many cases, the flexibility of the small group was lost: in others so-called 'free' worship settled into fixed patterns with very rare use of spiritual gifts, and — ironically — the new legalisms and controls rapidly became more rigid even than those of the old denominations.

5. Task/Question (By yourself)

Have you had a bruising experience of church life such as those outlined above? Whether you were one who left a church or one who stayed, it may have left a bitter taste and a desire in many cases to have nothing more to do with the issues — or even with the faith as a whole. Try to review the issues more dispassionately to gain a useful understanding of past injuries or errors and to be able to move on constructively.

*

Section 6

To return to my own experience of this movement at the University of Durham in the early seventies, I should begin by saying that there was an outreach mission being planned by Christian students to the university as a whole. A well-known church minister from York, named David Watson, was going to give various lectures with the overall title: 'My God is Real'. While preparations for this were under way, groups of students in the different colleges began to pray for its effectiveness, and I joined one such group in my own college.

There were about a dozen people present one day at this prayer group meeting, and we were praying together, taking turns to ask God's blessing on different aspects of the proposed mission. One of my college friends, Carol, took a turn and introduced her prayer with the words: 'I would like to share a few thoughts that have come to me.' Then she continued: 'Seek my face, my children, and I will pour out blessings on you.' It is hard to describe just how electrifying I — and several other group members — found these words to be. It was as if I had heard Jesus speaking straight to us. I had never heard his voice so directly before, but I recognised it instantly as that of the person I had been worshipping and serving all these years.

I do not mean that Carol put on a different voice or that she was taken over by the Spirit of Christ in the way that spiritualists claim a medium is possessed by the spirit of a person who has died. She remained herself and in control of what she was saying and yet her words were imbued with such power that they lifted the experience of prayer into a completely new dimension.

Afterwards I asked her about this and she and another friend, Dave, explained that she had been exercising the gift of prophesy, but because she knew we were not accustomed to its use, had introduced the message she felt she had been given by explaining that the thought of these words had come to her. The prophetic gift, she explained can come as direct words of God to his people; the 'thus says the Lord' of the Old Testament prophets. Its authenticity should be judged by the church depending on the degree to which the church is built up by the words uttered. Of course, a preacher can have his or her words informed by this gift of God's Spirit, but there was the possibility of its use in this more direct fashion, which Carol had demonstrated.

After this, I questioned Carol further on this issue of the Holy Spirit and she told me of her experiences which had begun before her college years, in the city of Hong Kong where she had been brought up, although she was not Chinese herself but of English extraction. To cut a long story short, I asked Carol and Dave to pray for me to be filled with the Holy Spirit, even though I fully understood that I would not be Christian at all if it had not been for the operation of the Holy Spirit in bringing Christ to birth in me, so to speak. It was a case of 'more of the same', rather than something alien to me.

6. Task/Question (Group/By yourself)

If you have had any experience of people exercising spiritual gifts in this way, select an occasion on which you found it helpful — or unhelpful — and give an account of it in spoken or written form. Try to give reasons for your response.

*

Section 7

I half expected to start babbling in tongues as soon as they prayed for me, but that didn't happen until about a year later when Carol prayed for me again and encouraged me to activate my voice rather than sit there with my mouth open waiting for something 'magic' to happen. What did happen at the time, however, was that I sensed the love of God for me in a deeper way than ever before and the fruit of the Spirit, which I felt I had looked for in vain in my own life, began to grow, as did my role as an encourager amongst my friends and family.

For example, I had struggled for several years with my own jealousy of one of my sisters and while reading the 'New English

Bible', one of the first of a series of modern translations of the Bible which were published around that time, I came across stories that I knew well but which I saw in a new light. The story of Jacob and Esau, for example and the story of the prodigal son were particularly helpful. I saw that my jealousy was quite unnecessary, as although my sister *was* a gifted and attractive person, that fact did not need to take anything away from my rather different contribution to life in general. I could enjoy her successes and not regard them as some kind of threat. The Spirit of Truth had come to my aid.

In fact, I discovered a deeper love for my sister and found I had something to offer her when she visited me in Durham and on subsequent occasions. In general I felt freer of selfish concerns and more able to take in the needs and issues which were troubling my friends and acquaintances. I would find a genuine love and concern moving me to reach out to others instead of thinking that I *ought* to have that motivation, but not finding it within me, even though I had usually tried to act in the best interests of the people I met. The loving Spirit of Christ was at work in conjunction with my own spirit to make a difference to those around me. I need not say what a blessedness this was after the lean years of despair.

What seems significant to me now about this period of my life, is that it was in facing up to my fear of the more obviously miraculous gifts, that I came to realise my need of God's Holy Spirit in order to demonstrate genuinely *any* of the fruit or gifts, whether apparently miraculous or not. In other words, it was quite outside my reach to display any of the qualities or abilities of the Christian life in my own strength. Everything had to be received. It is quite remarkable how long it took me to realise that no matter how hard I tried, no matter how many resolutions I made, I could not make myself into a good or an effective person. I had to yield control of my own efforts to God, something which I could only do in the end by going out of my depth and trusting him to save me. It felt very like Peter's experience of stepping out of the boat and walking towards Jesus on the water.

7. Task/Question (Group/By yourself)

This experience of the Charismatic Movement was appropriate to a person of my personality — that is, rather over-responsible and anxious by both nature and training. However, the Spirit of Truth would, no doubt, have different dealings with someone of a different personality. My experience as a school teacher has taught me that the same emphasis is not needed for all pupils. Perhaps you have an experience of God's Spirit that you could recount for your own or others' benefit.

*

Section 8

So what can the church do with this recovered knowledge of the workings of the Holy Spirit, when it has become in many circles such a byword for dissension and disorder? Paul's famous love chapter in Corinthians 13 outlines his strategy for dealing with something which also caused difficulties in the early church. His solution continues in chapter 14, where he urges the young churches to conduct themselves in an orderly way, using but not abusing the gifts of God. Not surprisingly, today's church also needs to learn how to exercise the gifts in a loving way, being considerate of both believers and unbelievers who may be present. The challenge of such a task should never be underestimated.

It can be helpful to compare these individual and corporate experiences with how messy a building site can be. Very frequently major demolition work is required before the new structure can be erected. Clouds of dust and debris make it an unpleasant place to be at times. Endless preparing of foundations and materials may make it seem as if no progress is being made at all. It is important that different parts of the work be carried out in the right order, so that decoration, for example, does not have to be repeated after being disturbed in order to put in central heating. Time and money can be wasted if careless or fraudulent workmen are employed. Many people have nightmare stories of cowboy builders running away with their life savings and leaving a house that is uninhabitable.

What, in these circumstances, can encourage people to continue with the project until its completion? Sometimes it is as basic as having no alternative. At other times regular discussions with the master builder will keep the house-owner informed of progress which may not be obvious, the prospect of a successful completion acting as a carrot to take him or her through the dark days. Experiments with poor workers can be written off as losses to be cut; effective alternatives can be found where there are problems with materials; the buzz of creating something beautiful and useful can be drawn on when exhaustion threatens and over-ambitious plans can be replaced with more realistic ones. Sometimes, especially in the case of the largest building projects, it is the second generation of owners who see the completion of the project, the first having died before it was finished, content to have played a part in the whole big picture.

The growth of the church is compared to the erection of a building in various places in the New Testament, for example; Paul, in 1 Corinthians 3: 9-17, explains that the church is *God's* building, and his people work only under his direction and only on the foundation of Jesus Christ. Each person's work will be inspected and will only last if done properly. Then, lest we run away with the idea that he is referring to the literal fabric of any building, he makes the point in verse 16:

> 'Don't you know that *you yourselves* are God's temple and that God's Spirit lives in you?' (*NIV* italics mine.)

Peter also uses the same image to describe the people of the church when, in his first letter, chapter 2, verse 5, he says:

> 'You...like living stones, are being built into a spiritual house' (*NIV*)

The emphasis has moved from the importance of the activity of Christians either individually or corporately attempting to build the church — even under the direction of God himself and on the foundation of Jesus Christ — to the importance of *the activity of God* in shaping and incorporating each Christian into the building that *he* is making.

8. Task/Question (Group)

Read 1 Chronicles 17 especially verses 4 and 10b. Here David sets out to build a house for God, but God checks his plans, reminding him that God has always chosen to meet with his people in temporary accommodation — the travelling tent of the wandering Israelites. By contrast, God undertakes to build a house for David instead, in the sense of a dynasty, and says that one of his descendants will have the job of building a permanent house for God. Can you suggest how this promise was fulfilled in both earthly and heavenly ways?

*

Section 9

Your answer will no doubt have included both Solomon, David's son, and Jesus, his more distant descendant. We have already considered the connection between Jesus and Solomon in the last three sections of Chapter 5, and it is appropriate to consider it further in connection with their common task of building a permanent house for God. Another famous reference in John's gospel comes into its own in this connection. Again it is taken from the farewell discourses between Jesus and his disciples, from John 14:1-3:

> 'Do not let your hearts be troubled. Trust in God; trust also in me.
> In my Father's house are many rooms; if it were not so, I would
> have told you. I am going there to prepare a place for you. And if
> I go and prepare a place for you, I will come back and take you to
> be with me that you also may be where I am.' (*NIV*)

Here Jesus uses the image of a huge house with many rooms to describe where God lives. He describes himself as the host making the house ready for his followers to come and live there with him and he promises to come and collect them when the time comes.

Just as the promise of God to David had both an earthly and a heavenly fulfilment, we might expect this promise of Jesus to be the same. There is something we can expect in this life as well as in the next. Jesus describes his Father's house as a very spacious place, with room for all his followers. Just as a host decides which room each guest should occupy, preparing the one most suitable for each person or group, so Jesus prepares a place for each individual and group of his disciples to occupy. The important point for each person and group is that they will be able to be with Jesus there.

This has an obvious application to the different earthly circumstances each individual or group finds themselves in. When discussing marital status, for example, Paul makes the following remarks:

> 'Don't be wishing you were someplace else or with someone else.
> Where you are right now is God's place for you. Live and obey and
> love and believe right there.' (1 Corinthians 7:17 *The Message*)

Later in the same chapter he qualifies these remarks a little, for example if someone is in an oppressive situation and has the chance to leave it, he or she should take the opportunity. However, the main point remains, that it is a matter of serving God in the present situation and circumstances, rather than trying to run around finding 'where it's at', as they say.

This attitude to church affiliation can also be quite constructive, a healthy counter to restless looking over the shoulder all the time. If and when God requires someone to be in a different place or situation, it will become clear. Trust in both God and in Christ is the key to not letting the heart be troubled, as Jesus pointed out.

9. Task/Question (By yourself)

Look around the 'room' that has been prepared for you in your earthly life. In what ways can you 'live and obey and love and believe' right where you are?

*

Section 10

There is also the possibility of a heavenly fulfilment of this promise of Jesus to his followers. In chapters 9 and 10 of his letter, the writer of Hebrews explains that the whole Jewish system of worship in the tent of God's presence and later in the temple building, was only a reflection or copy of a heavenly or spiritual reality in which Jesus played the part of both priest offering a sacrifice and the lamb being sacrificed. The purpose of the sacrifice was to remove the guilt of worshippers, so that they would be able to approach God boldly to ask for his help. When the literal tent or temple was in operation, the sacrifices had to be offered again and again as the guilt of God's people could not be finally dealt with by the sacrificing of animals.

However, Jesus' actions are so effective that they do not need to be repeated again and again. He can wait for what he has done to take full effect, confident that it will do so, completely and utterly. There will be a fulfilment of his promise to provide a place for his people, not only in their earthly lives, but also in the heavenly or spiritual dimension. What he gives now is a guarantee of what is to come.

This leads us back to the Holy Spirit as he is the one who makes the link between the earthly life and the heavenly one. This is spelt out quite specifically in a few places in the New Testament, for example in 2 Corinthians 1: 20-22:

> 'Whatever God has promised gets stamped with the Yes of Jesus.......God affirms us, making us a sure thing in Christ, putting his Yes within us. By his Spirit he has stamped us with his eternal

pledge — a sure beginning of what he is destined to complete.'
(*The Message*)

Or in Ephesians 1:13-14:

'It's in Christ that you, once you heard the truth and believed it (this Message of your salvation), found yourselves home free — signed, sealed, and delivered by the Holy Spirit. This signet from God is the first instalment on what's coming, a reminder that we'll get everything God has planned for us, a praising and glorious life.' (*The Message*)

The Holy Spirit, in this aspect of his work therefore, is the one who gives the followers of Jesus a taster of what they can expect in the heavenly life. He's the one who demonstrates that unbreakable hope is not simply 'pie in the sky when you die'. On the contrary, it is the assurance that what is to come is guaranteed by what is presently happening and is of the same order.

This experience of the work of the Holy Spirit has transformed life for me. Although the outer circumstances of my life since then have sometimes been very difficult, the difficulties have seemed as nothing when compared to the days of powerlessness before I knew about the work of God's Spirit to any great degree. The difference is that I now have a sense of that inner source which will not fail me whatever happens. It is this inner life which sustains and feeds the hope that outward circumstances will eventually yield to the lordship of Christ in both this life and the next.

10. Task/Question (Group)
Make a study of the wonderful eighth chapter of Romans where you will find Paul's description of and celebration of this truth.

Chapter 8: A Time of Amnesty

Section 1

The time has come to turn our minds to the future aspect of unbreakable hope. Until now we have been considering how such hope may affect our present lives and the lives of others with whom we share the planet — and quite rightly too, because any hope of heaven which did not have an impact on our earthly lives would have lost touch with the whole of reality, and to that extent would be suspect and open to the charge of escapism.

Not only that, but unscrupulous leaders, both religious and secular, have sometimes cynically used the religious belief of oppressed people to keep them subservient or 'in their place', which of course is a travesty of the purpose and nature of the hope of heaven. In such cases religion has indeed been 'the opium of the people' as Karl Marx claimed. Suffering people have been encouraged to endure rather than resist oppression, with the promise that all will be bliss when they die. Any hope of heaven which entails making less effort to obtain justice here and now is not the unbreakable hope we are studying, but some sort of opt out from proper responsibility and engagement with the world.

On the contrary, true hope for the life to come has the opposite effect upon those who exercise it. In other words, people who are convinced that Jesus is indeed preparing a place for them in his father's house — to use the words we looked at from the beginning of chapter 14 of John's gospel — should themselves be more able to be free from the fear of death. They should be more able to be free from the need to amass great worldly wealth or to worry unduly about their reputations or to want everything to go their own way. They have themselves discovered a profound acceptance and in gratitude, seek to serve the one who accepted them by showing the same concern for the welfare of others. Of course, the hope of heaven is not fully worked out in the lives of many believers, but the essential elements are there for potential development.

So what exactly is promised about the life to come? This is not as straightforward as it may at first appear because the biblical material concerning it takes many forms. As well as Jesus' own statements in the gospels about what is to come, there are various references to the end times in the letters of the New Testament and finally in the apocalyptic writing of Revelation, which has generated all sorts of weird and wonderful interpretations and detailed timetables of events which are said to be due at the end of history. Just as it was not clear to the Jews at the time of Jesus quite how Jesus was the fulfilment of Old Testament prophecies, so we, as we look forward, cannot anticipate exactly how things will be, not only in our own personal futures, but in the world as a whole.

In the scientific world, there is also a great deal of uncertainty about the future of our planet. Those concerned about the environment claim — with some fairly convincing evidence — that global warming is occurring at an unprecedented rate, largely as a result of human activity, and they advocate specific measures we should all take to reduce our harm to the world. Cooperation between nations is urged as a global approach is required.

Economically, the future also looks very uncertain at the moment, with markets collapsing and financial institutions having to be bailed out by massive injections of government or taxpayers' money. Many people are facing unemployment, the repossession of their houses or the failure of their businesses. As usual, those who are least able to cope with the financial pressures are often the ones on whom the burden falls most heavily, while those who seem to have caused the problem walk away with swollen pension funds protected by legal contracts which were made before the issues were clear. Again, many world leaders are seeking global solutions as it is more obvious than ever that what affects one nation very quickly affects others.

1. Task/Question (Group/By yourself)

What are your feelings when you consider some of the terrible exploitation in our world: for example, the exploitation of religious belief, the environment or the financial systems of the world?

If you were God, what would you want to do about these things?

*

Section 2

There is a wonderful poem imagining such a scenario by the north-eastern Scottish poet Charles Murray. I know not everyone will be able to fathom the Doric dialect, but for those who do, it is worth quoting in full:

'Gin I was God'

Gin I was God, sittin' up there abeen,
Weariet nae doot noo a' my darg was deen,
Deaved wi' the harps an' hymns oonendin' ringin',
Tired o' the flockin' angels hairse wi' singin',
To some clood-edge I'd daunder furth an' feth,
Look ower an' watch hoo things were gyaun aneth,
Syne, gin I saw hoo men I'd made mysel'
Had startit in to pooshan, sheet an' fell,
To reive an' rape, an' fairly mak' a hell
O' my braw birlin' Earth. — a hale week's wark —
I'd cast my coat again, rowe up my sark,
An' or they'd time to lench a second ark,
Tak' back my word an sen' anither spate,
Droon oot the hale hypothec, dicht the sklate,
Own my mistak', an', aince I'd cleared the brod,
Start a'thing ower again, gin I was God.

Murray imagines that if he were God, he would give up on his spoiled world, send another flood and destroy it all in order to make a completely new start. As I read and appreciate this satisfying poem in all its comic seriousness, I realise the difference between the exasperation of a good man who considers the ills of the world, and the patience of God himself, who has not yet brought down the curtain on his 'braw birlin' Earth' in this way.

Often, as we consider these issues connected with injustice, we can feel a sort of rage at the unfairness of it all: we tremble for the future of our planet, we have a longing for the vindication of people of integrity, an anguish about the victims of history, an urgent desire for justice to prevail at last and for the bullies, the exploiters, the devious, the negligent and the fat cats to have the tables turned on them. A true 'hunger and thirst for righteousness', as the Bible describes it, is the engine by which greater justice can actively be sought.

A famous example is the work done by the Muslim economist, Mohammed Yunus, the Nobel peace prize winner, who became 'Banker to the Poor' of Bangladesh, especially the women. As he describes in his autobiography of that name, he lent them small amounts without requiring collateral, and when they repaid the loan, they became eligible for larger amounts. His system has been hugely successful and has been copied in many countries of the world, lifting millions of women — and therefore whole families —

out of the direst poverty. In these days of banking scandal, his story is testimony to what can be done if the will is there.

2. Task/Question (Group/By yourself)

Can we embrace such an altruistic and demanding ambition or will we succumb to the temptation to become armchair critics of the exploits of public figures; will we turn into whingers or people with great chips on their shoulders and allow bitterness to characterise all our attitudes and conversations?

*

Section 3

At this point, another major, though sometimes unpopular, doctrine of the faith can come to our aid. It is the doctrine of God's judgement. The God in whom there is no darkness at all cannot let people 'get away with' relentless cruelty, greed, criminal carelessness and exploitation. There has to be a day of reckoning, when the record of wrongs is 'read out' and judgement is pronounced, when restoration is made, when injuries and hurts are healed, when vindication of right and good behaviour takes place and evil behaviour is punished.

Belief in such a day, whatever form it may take, is both a biblical and a necessary ingredient in the outlook of a person who is able to see the injustices in the world without losing hope that they will be put right thoroughly and publicly. Psalm 73 is a wonderful meditation on this very subject. The psalmist admits very honestly:

> 'I envied the arrogant when I saw the prosperity of the wicked.'
> (Verse 3)

He wonders about the value of his own efforts and those of others who tried to live fairly:

> 'Surely in vain have I kept my heart pure: in vain have I washed my hands in innocence.' (Verse13)

He explains what saved him from bitterness of heart:

> 'When I tried to understand all this, it was oppressive to me till I entered the sanctuary of God; then I understood their final destiny. Surely you place them on slippery ground: you cast them down to ruin.' (Verses16-18, all *NIV*)

The psalmist ends with the recollection that his best reward in any case is being in tune with God's character and living in harmony with him. A more appropriate attitude to wrongdoers is to pity them for being so far from God, which in itself is a kind of judgement, quite apart from any future reckoning when they themselves will see the horror of what they have done. (For more on living generously, please see the end of Section 9.)

Think of a person — or a group of people — whose evil actions or lack of action has caused untold distress to yourself or others, and who has obviously, so far, felt little or no remorse or regret about this fact. Picture that person — or people — at the moment of death, or before God's judgement seat, being faced with what they have done when it is too late to make any kind of restitution and when there is no way of hiding the truth or fudging the issue.

Such an understanding of God's judgement can alleviate our bitter feelings towards evildoers, and help us to focus more on restoring justice for the sake of the oppressed, rather than expending energy on desiring revenge, because the oppressors are God's responsibility. As Paul reminded the Romans in chapter 12 of his letter, at verse 19:

> 'Don't insist on getting even; that's not for you to do. 'I'll do the judging,' says God. 'I'll take care of it'. (*The Message*)

and in case we think he'll be too lenient with them, the writer of Hebrews tells us in chapter 10, verse 31:

> 'It is a dreadful thing to fall into the hands of the living God' (*NIV*)

and in chapter 12, verse 29:

> 'For our God is a consuming fire.' (*NIV*)

3. Task/Question (Group)

Although the Bible discourages the seeking of revenge for its own sake, it includes many stories of brave people who challenge oppressive power at great risk to themselves. Can you think of any examples, either from the biblical texts or from history or contemporary life?

*

Section 4

I'm sure you will have realised the corollary to a belief in this aspect of the judgement of God. It is, of course, that, lest we become too complacent in considering the judgement of others, we need to remember that we ourselves will also be judged by the same God. In fact, just as the Holy Spirit gives Christ's followers a taster of the life to come with regard to matters of salvation, so he gives them a taster of the life to come in connection with God's judgement. In this case, it is by way of being a warning, so that they may take steps to make the necessary changes in their lives while they still can. This is referred to in the first letter of Peter, chapter 4 at verse 17:

'It's judgement time for Christians. We're first in line.' (*The Message*)

Paul also refers to this process in connection with the Corinthian church, some of whom were not taking the act of communion seriously, failing to remember what Christ had done for them. He urged them to engage in self examination before taking the bread and wine of the communion, so that they would not incur God's judgement in the shape of weakness or sickness, and Paul goes on to say:

'If we get this straight now, we won't have to be straightened out later on. Better to be confronted by the Master now than to face a fiery confrontation later.' (1 Corinthians 11:32 *The Message*)

This process should be reassuring to all who honestly want truth to prevail in their own and other people's lives. Just as wrongdoing by the unscrupulous will be judged fairly and the offenders held to account, so wrongdoing by those who profess to follow Christ as well as those we might consider 'good' people will not be overlooked either. It is not possible for anyone to deceive God. All wrongdoing must either be confessed and forgiven on the basis of Christ's sacrifice, and the necessary life changes made, or it will be subject to judgement. This is the orthodox Christian position with regard to God's judgement.

4. Task/Question (Group)
In what way can this understanding of God's judgement enhance unbreakable hope for both our own futures and the future of the world as a whole? Try to sum up the benefits in a sentence or two.

Section 5

One of the hazards in considering the judgement of God is in making crass equivalences between particular tragedies and particular offences. Jesus had something to say about the misapprehensions that can abound in this area. In the gospel of Luke at the beginning of chapter 13, he refers to two tragedies which had taken place recently in Israel at that time: Pilate had murdered some Galileans who were offering sacrifices at the Temple, and the Tower of Siloam had fallen on eighteen people who were crushed and killed. Referring to those who had been killed, Jesus said to the crowd who were listening to him:

> 'Do you think they were more guilty than all the others living in Jerusalem? I tell you, no! But unless you repent, you too will all perish' (verse 4b *NIV*)

His attitude therefore was that these tragedies were not a punitive demonstration of how evil the victims were, but should be used as a wake-up call to remind others that death can come at any time and they should make themselves ready to meet their own final judgement. He then went on to tell the story of a fruit tree that failed to bear any fruit and the owner asked the gardener to chop it down. The gardener asked for another year to tend the tree in the hope that it would bear fruit before putting the axe to it.

This idea of a merciful stay of execution crops up again in the third chapter of Peter's second letter. He refers to Jesus' promise to return, an event which the early church tended to think might be imminent. The fact that it was not happening had caused some people to become complacent and to think that it would not happen at all. This passage is worth quoting at length, as it outlines the logic of the delay as some saw it:

> 'Don't overlook the obvious here, friends. With God, one day is as good as a thousand years, a thousand years as a day. God isn't late with his promise as some measure lateness. He is restraining himself on account of you, holding back the End because he doesn't want anyone lost. He's giving everyone space and time to change. But when the Day of God's Judgement does come, it will be unannounced, like a thief. The sky will collapse with a thunderous bang, everything disintegrating in a huge

conflagration, earth and all its works exposed to the scrutiny of Judgement.

Since everything here today might well be gone tomorrow, do you see how essential it is to live a holy life? Daily expect the Day of God, eager for its arrival. The galaxies will burn up and the elements melt down that day — but we'll hardly notice. We'll be looking the other way, ready for the promised new heavens and the promised new earth, all landscaped with righteousness.

So my dear friends, since this is what you have to look forward to, do your very best to be found living at your best, in purity and peace. Interpret our Master's patient restraint for what it is: salvation.' (Verses 8 — 15 *The Message*)

Looking forward to the day of judgement was to be the attitude of Christ's followers as it would bring ultimate satisfaction to those who hunger and thirst for righteousness, according to Christ's promise in one of the beatitudes in Matthew 5: 6. Not only that, but it would encourage his disciples to be at their best all the time as they had no idea when the end would be.

5. Task/Question (Group)

What do you think of those groups of people who do things such as going up to the top of a high mountain because they believe the end of the world is coming on a particular date which they have identified by, for example, looking at certain passages of apocalyptic writing? Read Matthew 24: 36 for Jesus' take on this question.

*

Section 6

Anyone who claims to know when the end of the world will be is deceiving himself, according to Jesus. He didn't even know that himself: only God the Father knows. One of that day's often repeated characteristics is that it will come unexpectedly. The purpose of this is that people should keep themselves in a state of readiness and not engage in anything which would make them ashamed before him at his coming, but rather be found doing his compassionate and constructive work in whatever shape they have been given it to do. Part of the discourse is the famous story of the sheep and the goats, (Matthew 25:31 — 46) a parable about the judgement of people who would be separated out according to whether they had cared for the unfortunate of the world.

The whole of Matthew chapters 24 and 25 contain Jesus' comments about the future, both the immediate future involving the fall of Jerusalem — which took place in AD 70 — and the more distant future when he himself promised to return in an unmistakable way. Verse 30 of chapter 24 describes this event in no uncertain terms:

'The Arrival of the Son of Man....will fill the skies — no-one will miss it. Unready people all over the world, outsiders to the splendour and power, will raise a huge lament as they watch the Son of Man blazing out of heaven.' (*The Message*)

This is obviously an event that has not yet happened, and Jesus said it would follow a time of trouble on an unprecedented scale, which nobody would survive unless the time were cut short, which he promised it would be. To exercise unbreakable hope, therefore, we must take into account this time of great trouble without wavering, knowing that the opposition to God's activity on earth has been, is and will be very fierce at certain times. To be forewarned in this matter is to be forearmed:

'Keep your head and don't panic,'

is Jesus' advice (chapter 24: 6 *The Message*). There are also quite frequent warnings against deceivers who will claim to know all about what is happening and spread false rumours about Jesus' return. He urges his followers not to be foolish and to keep their wits about them:

'Staying with it — that's what God requires. Stay with it to the end. You won't be sorry, and you'll be saved. All during this time, the good news — the Message of the kingdom — will be preached all over the world, a witness staked out in every country. And then the end will come.' (Chapter 24:14 *The Message*)

6. Task/Question (Group)
Can you suggest any purposes that the long wait through times of trouble might serve? Look at the other parables in Matthew 25:1-30 for some ideas.

*

Section 7

Another of the purposes for the delay, according to Jesus' remarks in the previous chapter — Matthew 24 — was that there would be time for the message about God's kingdom to spread throughout the world. Everyone was to have a chance to hear it and respond to it.

When I was a school teacher, I regularly required homework to be handed in by a certain date. If the deadline were not met and the child showed concern about the matter, I would sometimes allow a period of grace, setting a new deadline for the work to be done, before resorting to sanctions. The Christian understanding of this era since the life, death and resurrection of Christ, is that it is such a period of grace or amnesty, a time when people may prepare themselves for eternity, may discover the provisions that have been made for them by the work of Christ and avail themselves of them.

It is also clear, from various passages in the Bible, that those who have not heard the Message of God's kingdom specifically will also be treated fairly according to what they *do* know. For example in Romans 2: 14 — 16, Paul makes the following statement:

> 'When outsiders who have never heard of God's law follow it more or less by instinct, they confirm its truth by their obedience. They show that God's law is not something alien, imposed on us from without, but woven into the very fabric of our creation. There is something deep within them that echoes God's yes and no, right and wrong. Their response to God's yes and no will become public knowledge on the day God makes his final decision about every man and woman. The Message from God that I proclaim through Jesus Christ takes into account all these differences.' (*The Message*)

There is room therefore, according to this passage, for everyone to be judged fairly by the God in whom there is no darkness at all.

However, I doubt that any one of us would feel quite secure if we knew we would be judged simply with fairness and justice. The older we are, the more we become aware of the need for someone to be rooting for us, giving us the benefit of the doubt, forgiving our lapses, looking for the intention of the heart, rather than the patchy achievement. In other words, we feel the need for the mercy and love of God, the need for him to make up for our lack, to make good our shortfall, to take our paltry loaves and fish, and make them into the feast for the needy that is required.

The good news of God's kingdom contains all these elements, as well as the rigour that keeps us on our toes and challenges us to grow up. In this context, the foretaste of God's judgement for Christ's followers can in fact be seen rather as the discipline of the Holy Spirit. It is like the difference between the punitive aspects of a prison sentence and the chance for rehabilitation that can and should be offered to those in prison.

7. Task/Question (Group)
Read Hebrews 12: 5 — 11 for a way of looking at hardship in terms of God's discipline.

*

Section 8

An Experience of the Discipline of the Holy Spirit
An example from my own experience may be relevant at this point and I should like to recount an incident which helped me to absorb the teaching about rest which appears in chapter 4 of the study.

In the early seventies, I was a young secondary school teacher in my first post in a large state school in a small country town. The school was not as difficult a place to work as some of the big city schools, but for me, it was something of a baptism of fire. At the time, the school leaving age was sixteen and some of the most difficult classes were classes of leavers, who were not planning to take any more public exams. Most of them did not want to be there and had no motive to work or cooperate with a young and inexperienced teacher trying to teach them English or Religious Education.

As most newly qualified teachers of the time discovered, teaching a full timetable was a hugely onerous task with so little experience to draw on. Most evenings, I was working into the small hours of the next morning, preparing for the next day and marking work to be returned to the pupils. During the day, much of the time was spent struggling with unruly classes or trying to get ahead with the marking and preparation. At four o'clock, I was wrung out and staggered home to begin the whole process all over again. It would only be possible to do it when young, idealistic and energetic!

During the holidays I became involved in some of the Summer Missions that were so popular at that time. I found them hugely enjoyable, as many people of roughly my own age converged on a seaside town to run children's work on beaches and evening youth events, to visit the housing schemes and take part in church services on the Sundays. As you may have noticed, it was something of a busman's holiday for me, although the team effort made it seem so much easier than school teaching.

One particular summer, during which I spent two of my six weeks' holiday in such a way, I was asked by a school club leader to devote another fortnight of my holiday helping to run a camp for the club. When I was asked to do it, my heart sank, as I saw my precious holiday being eaten up by activities, yet because I had a gap in my diary at the time, I felt I could hardly refuse to undertake such a worthwhile project, so I agreed and did it, and as is often the case, it was quite enjoyable, once I got down to it.

However, as was no doubt inevitable, by the time the school year began again, I was not properly rested and struggled to keep going, concerned that I felt so weary when it was only September. Shortly before the October holiday, I finally realised I was ill and was diagnosed with the dreaded glandular fever. True to form, it dragged on until Christmas and recurred a couple of times later in the year, which meant that my colleagues in the department and a number of supply teachers had to pick up the tab for me in a way I would not have wished on them.

I recount this long story because during the time I had off work, I had much time to think it all over and asked in my prayers for understanding of the experience. I learned several lessons from it all, the most important being that an empty space in a diary does not necessarily mean that I can cope with taking on anything anyone else thinks I should do to fill it. Since that time, I have learned to take note of that sinking of the heart when an excessive demand is being made on my time, and to refuse it. Occasionally I have ignored the warning and invariably become ill if I do.

The experience of glandular fever I now regard as extremely valuable to me in the conduct of my life. I regard it as a boundary put in place by the Holy Spirit, which enables me to steward my time and energies effectively and to take proper control of my life.

8. Task/Question (By yourself)
In the light of this account, can you identify anything in your own experience which could be the training of God's Holy Spirit?

*

Section 9

In case the idea of being disciplined by God himself seems too scary, it is worth considering that one who sees all the circumstances of our lives and experiences will be able to tailor the discipline to the need of each individual more successfully than any parent or teacher, who has to be seen to be consistent, whatever the character or sensitivities of the individual child. As King David pointed out in one of his psalms of thanks for God's deliverance from danger:

> 'To the pure you show yourself pure, but to the crooked you show yourself shrewd.' (Psalm 18:26 *NIV*)

or as a well known translation of a French proverb has it:

> 'God tempers the wind to the shorn lamb' (This form of words appears in a narrative of the eighteenth century author, Laurence Sterne: *A Sentimental Journey through France and Italy*)

In other words, the Holy Spirit knows just how much pressure to apply to maximise our chance of learning necessary lessons, though never taking away our ability to refuse the lessons if we determine to do so.

It may be worth establishing — as we consider this issue — that interpreting some of life's trials as the training of the Holy Spirit does not preclude a clear grasp of the fact that there are natural and scientific reasons for difficult experiences that come to us: illness, for instance, is often caused by bacteria which invade our systems; accidents can be caused by careless driving and so on. These causes can and should be explored by those who are qualified to do so, with a view to minimising their bad effects in our own lives and those of others. However, looking beneath the surface to the significance of such events in God's purposes for our lives is a way of being able to make capital out of a reversal, a way of turning a tragedy into a stepping stone in our pilgrimage of hope.

If this sounds too easy and glib, we only have to look at Jesus' agony as he contemplated and then suffered the horror of crucifixion, to realise that God is not callously ordering our experiences from a distance. He is sweating it out with us at every step. To make a crucifixion into a means of universal salvation shows the mighty power of God to transform disaster into a vehicle of wholeness.

The one in whom there is no darkness at all is really the only person from whom it is endurable to learn life's hardest lessons. There is no patronising superiority, no crushing harshness, no bullying or unfair pressurising, no cruel mockery or scorn; we are not filled with nameless fear or given a sense of vague unspecified guilt, nor any feeling of being worthless or hopeless. In fact, if we experience any of these negative attitudes or results, we can be sure that they do not come from the one in whom there is no darkness at all and therefore we may safely banish them and listen for a deeper voice.

What we find, beneath the voices of condemnation and discouragement, is an infinite patience, a delight in every little step of progress we make, an imaginative presentation of the facts of our situation to us that enables us to see what we can do to change, a sense of being understood more profoundly than we understand ourselves, a sense of someone great and awe-inspiring approaching us, taking the time and trouble to consider our little concerns and to address them in ways that do not make us feel worthless or useless, but that show us where we can make a difference. We have a sense of privilege, a sense that we are being allowed into the community of people whose lives are blessed by God.

At the same time, if we have the cheek to become complacent, or to justify ourselves stridently, suppressing our deepest certainties, we can sometimes find a deafening silence in the space where the still small voice is usually to be found. We may be brought up short by a sudden reversal, a wake-up call or reality check that gives us another chance to recalibrate our approach to life in a more honest way.

9. Task/Question (By yourself)

How sensitive to the nudgings of reality do you consider yourself to be? Ask a trusted friend for his or her honest opinion and promise not to react defensively if there is anything challenging in it.

*

Section 10

In examining hardships in terms of the discipline of the Holy Spirit, I do not in any way mean to suggest that people who suffer a great deal are more guilty than average. That really would be rubbing salt in the wound. It was something that Job's comforters did while their supposed friend was going through terrible times, adding to his distress and frustration considerably. The account of his experiences is to be found in the Old Testament book which bears his name. Although the date of its writing is unknown, it is an early book and describes a man who lived around the time of Abraham, that is, approximately 1800 BC.

Some of the opening of Job's story is worth looking at in this connection, as it tackles the issue of whether God has favourites whom he protects unfairly from life's vicissitudes. The author imagines a conversation between God and Satan — the angel who tried to usurp God's authority, according to the Bible — in which Satan brought a complaint against Job. This idea of Satan being the voice of accusation has passed into our very language as we talk about 'playing the devil's advocate' in situations where we state the case against someone. Verses 8 — 12a of chapter 1 come over powerfully in *The Message*:

> 'God said to Satan, 'Have you noticed my friend Job? There's no one quite like him — honest and true to his word, totally devoted to God and hating evil.'
> Satan retorted, 'So you think Job does all that out of the sheer goodness of his heart? Why, no one ever had it so good! You pamper him like a pet, make sure nothing bad ever happens to him or his family or his possessions, bless him in everything he does — he can't lose! But what do you think would happen if you reached down and took away everything that is his? He'd curse you right to your face, that's what.'
> God replied, 'We'll see. Go ahead — do what you want with all that is his.'

When Job passed this test, Satan proposed another, involving the health of Job's own body, as well as his family and possessions, and the rest of the book explores Job's responses to the calamities that have come upon him as well as the advice of his friends.

The point here is that God allowed Satan to inflict trouble upon Job — not because he was a bad man, but precisely because he was a good man, so that the accusation of favouritism levelled against God could be shown to be hollow, and so that Job's goodness could be shown to be genuine and not simply 'cupboard love' as we call self-interested good behaviour. Most of his friends had to ask his pardon for suggesting that he had suffered because of wrongdoing. After arguing his case with God and hearing his answers, Job learned a new humility before the mysteries of God, recognising the limits of our understanding of God's purposes, but realising their greatness.

One of Job's friends was more helpful to him in this process, the young man Elihu, who waited until the older men had had their say, and then, seeing that they had nothing relevant to offer, himself challenged and encouraged Job in a more constructive way. One of his statements is particularly helpful in facing hardship:

'Those who learn from their suffering, God delivers from their suffering.' (Job 36:15 *The Message*)

This point about God not having favourites is referred to by Jesus also, in the context of his difficult teaching on loving enemies.

'You're familiar with the old written law, 'Love your friend,' and its unwritten companion, 'Hate your enemy.' I'm challenging that. I'm telling you to love your enemies. Let them bring out the best in you, not the worst. When someone gives you a hard time, respond with the energies of prayer, for then you are working out of your true selves, your God-created selves. *This is what God does. He gives his best — the sun to warm and the rain to nourish — to everyone, regardless: the good and bad, the nice and nasty.* If all you do is love the lovable, do you expect a bonus? Anybody can do that. If you simply say hello to those who greet you, do you expect a medal? Any run-of-the-mill sinner does that.
In a word, what I'm saying is, 'Grow up.' You're kingdom subjects. Now live like it. Live out your God-created identity. Live generously and graciously toward others, the way God lives toward you.' (Matthew 5: 43-48 *The Message*, italics mine)

10. Task/Question (Group)
According to this passage, how can I legitimately make good use of my enemies? Try to sum up the ways in which reversals can be used to support unbreakable hope. The connection with character already explored may be relevant here.

I'd like to end this chapter with a verse composed by Charles, Baron Bowen, 1835-94, which acknowledges in a light-hearted way the cost of trying to maintain integrity in a corrupt world:

'The rain it raineth on the just
And also on the unjust fella:
But chiefly on the just, because
The unjust steals the just's umbrella.'

Chapter 9: A New Heaven and a New Earth

Section 1

Having looked at how we may maintain unbreakable hope in the face of — and in fact *because* of — the difficult concept of the judgement of God, let us turn to other aspects of the future elements of this hope, both for ourselves and for the whole creation.

According to parts of the great eighth chapter of Romans, mentioned at the end of Chapter 7 of this study, the created universe is portrayed as 'waiting' longingly to see humankind made whole, because it will then be able to become whole itself. The relevant verses are 19-22 and are worth quoting in full because of the close link they maintain between ourselves and the rest of the created world:

> 'For all creation is waiting patiently and hopefully for that future day when God will resurrect his children. On that day, thorns and thistles, sin, death and decay — the things that overcame the world against its will at God's command — will all disappear, and the world around us will share in the glorious freedom from sin which God's children enjoy.
> For we know that even the things of nature, like animals and plants, suffer in sickness and death, but these are 'labour pains' as they await this great event'
> (*The Living Bible*, a paraphrased translation of the ancient texts.)

This change in both human beings and nature which is promised in various places in the Bible is often described as the creation of 'a new heaven and a new earth'.

In the first creation, according to the author of Genesis, when human beings decided to ignore God's clearly understood guidelines, the consequences included enmity between certain creatures and people; painful childbearing; strife between the sexes; hard labour on the land to obtain enough food because of weeds and thistles — by implication the difficulties and problems of work in general — and finally, death to end it all. It was not long however, before promises of restoration were given. With Abraham, God began the long, painstaking process of undoing the harm that had been done to both human beings and nature.

In the new creation, God's children, according to the passage in Romans quoted above, enjoy a 'glorious freedom from sin'. Imagine a situation in which we have no temptation to overindulge ourselves: no temptation to be mean or selfish, but our whole delight is to do what God wants most for us: to love him and one another extravagantly. This is one of the experiences of which a foretaste is given to us in the present by the operation of the Holy Spirit with our own spirits. The promise we have been given is that this freedom will be fully realised in the resurrection life.

One of the earliest descriptions of the new heaven and the new earth was given by the prophet Isaiah, who was active in Jerusalem in the eighth century BC, at a time when the nation was in decline and being threatened by the Assyrian Empire. Isaiah was able to see beyond the terrible things that were happening to a time when his people's fortunes would be reversed and they would be re-established as a nation in their own land after a long period of exile. This return took place at the end of the sixth century BC and in the following years. Some of Isaiah's prophecies seem to have an even longer reach and describe how the whole world will benefit from the intervention of the greatest of the descendants of King David. He will right all wrongs and establish a new order altogether. The harmony of his reign is characterised in one of Isaiah's best known prophecies:

'The wolf will live with the lamb,
   the leopard will lie down with the goat,
the calf and the lion and the yearling together;
   and a little child will lead them.
The cow will feed with the bear,
   their young will lie down together,
   and the lion will eat straw like the ox.
The infant will play near the hole of the cobra,
   and the young child put his hand into the viper's nest.
They will neither harm nor destroy
   on all my holy mountain,
for the earth will be full of the knowledge of the Lord
   as the waters cover the sea.' (Isaiah 11:6 — 9, *NIV*)

1. Task/Question (By yourself)

Spend some time visualising such a scenario. Think of a beautiful natural scene, perhaps one you are familiar with, and fill it with the creatures and children of your choice. You might prefer to depict it in poetry, painting or photography or to use any of these art forms created by others. Leave space so that you may add to it as your understanding deepens.

*

Section 2

In the biblical descriptions of the new heaven and the new earth, as well as imagery of beautiful countryside — pastoral scenes and mountains — there is also much imagery of the perfect city which is called 'the new Jerusalem'. If we look at the whole biblical picture, it is clear that this is not always the same as the geographical Jerusalem we can visit if we go to Israel, any more than the biblical Egypt and Babylon, the places of slavery and exile, are the same as today's country of Egypt or today's town of Babylon, which is near Baghdad. Because of the experiences of the Hebrew people, these places came to have a symbolic significance for them which we need to explore if we are not to make literalist errors of understanding about them. What began as a particular place in the history of the Jews later assumed a more universal significance for the whole of God's people, including the Jews.

The hill on which the city of Jerusalem sits, Mount Zion, was known as the mountain of the Lord because the Temple which was the centre of Jewish worship for many years had been built there. In the depictions of the new heaven and the new earth, this mountain and city were taken up as imagery in an attempt to describe the indescribable. Isaiah frequently uses such imagery to portray his great vision of how the reign of God will be shown to everyone. In chapter 2, verses 2-4, we find these words:

> 'There's a day coming
>   when the mountain of God's House
> Will be The Mountain —
>   solid, towering over all mountains.
> All nations will river toward it,
>   people from all over set out for it.
> They'll say, 'Come',
>   let's climb God's mountain,
>   go to the House of the God of Jacob.
> He'll show us the way he works
>   so we can live the way we're made.'
> Zion's the source of the revelation.
>   God's Message comes from Jerusalem.
> He'll settle things fairly between nations.

133

He'll make things right between many peoples.
They'll turn their swords into shovels,
    their spears into hoes.
No more will nation fight nation;
    they won't play war any more.' (*The Message*)

In saying that Zion is the source of the revelation, Isaiah is endorsing the promise of God to Abraham, that it would be through his descendants that God would bring blessing and wholeness to the world. All the nations of the world are here depicted as streaming into the city of Jerusalem and abandoning their wars with one another. Isaiah expands on this picture in chapter 25 of his prophecy, verses 6-8:

'Here on this mountain, God-of-the-Angel-Armies
    will throw a feast for all the people of the world,
A feast of the finest foods, a feast with vintage wines,
    a feast of seven courses, a feast lavish with gourmet desserts.
And here on this mountain, God will banish
    the pall of doom hanging over all peoples,
The shadow of doom darkening all nations.
    Yes, he'll banish death forever.
And God will wipe the tears from every face.
    He'll remove every sign of disgrace
From his people, wherever they are.
    Yes! God says so! (*The Message*)

This passage also introduces us to another image of the new heaven and the new earth; that of a great feast or banquet. The New Testament takes this up as the marriage feast of the Lamb, the celebration when Christ and his people are finally made one. The celebration of the Lord's Supper instituted by Jesus is a kind of promise of what is to come in this regard. Jesus' words about this are recorded in Luke 22:15-16:

'You've no idea how much I have looked forward to eating this
Passover meal with you before I enter my time of suffering. It's
the last one I'll eat *until we all eat it together in the kingdom of
God*.' (*The Message* italics mine.)

2. Task/Question (By yourself)
Take some time to explore this image of the great celebratory feast at which God himself is host. Visualise or depict this scene.

Again use any of the arts to help you and be ready to add to it as and when you become aware of each new aspect of it. A well-loved poem entitled *Love* by George Herbert, for example, takes up the notion of a feast where God himself is host. Revelation 19:5-9 may be useful in various ways; for example, it suggests sounds and music which you could add to your vision of this great event if you wish.

*

Section 3

If 'the new Jerusalem' is not simply the geographical city of Jerusalem in Israel, then what is it? Isaiah is helpful here also. In the 65th chapter of his prophecy, we read these words in verses 17-19:

> 'Behold I will create
>   new heavens and a new earth.
> The former things will not be remembered,
>   nor will they come to mind.
> But be glad and rejoice for ever
>   in what I will create,
> for I will create Jerusalem to be a delight
>   and its people a joy.
> I will rejoice over Jerusalem
>   and take delight in my people;
> the sound of weeping and of crying
>   will be heard in it no more.' (*NIV*)

There is an obvious equivalence in this passage between the new Jerusalem and God's people, who think of themselves as his new creation. In the next and final chapter of Isaiah, chapter 66, verses 10-13, this picture is developed into one of a nursing mother:

> 'Rejoice, Jerusalem,
>   and all who love her, celebrate!
> And all you who have shed tears over her,
>   join in the happy singing.
> You newborns can satisfy yourselves
>   at her nurturing breasts.
> Yes, delight yourselves and drink your fill
>   at her ample bosom.'

God's Message:

> 'I'll pour robust well-being into her like a river,
>   the glory of nations like a river in flood.
> You'll nurse at her breasts,
>   nestle in her bosom,
>   and be bounced on her knees.
> As a mother comforts her child,
>   so I'll comfort you.
>   You will be comforted in Jerusalem.' (*The Message*)

This prophecy seems to relate to more than simply the 'old' Jerusalem. A similar development is suggested by Jesus' grief over the city of Jerusalem in his own day, which failed to recognise him as God's representative, coming to save it. He also used the image of a mother protecting her young as recorded in Luke 13:34:

> 'O Jerusalem, Jerusalem, you who killed the prophets and stone those sent to you, how often I have longed to gather your children together, as a hen gathers her chicks under her wings, but you were not willing!' (*NIV*)

An amazing aspect of the promise we are considering is that heaven as well as earth is to be made new. Could this mean that it will fulfil the longing in the heart of God himself, as well as the longings in our own hearts? If so, how far this is from the distant and impassive deity sometimes imagined by us. A closer look at the biblical texts reveals no such distant God, as is shown by Jesus' openly expressed longing in the verses quoted above from Luke.

The simple fact of being Jewish never was a guarantee that any group of people were truly God's people. The option of being 'not willing' was always open to them. They were always free to wriggle out from under the protection of his wings and go it alone, to distance themselves from their God and deny their heritage, or — at the very least — fail to recognise Jesus as their expected Messiah. Although Jesus wept over Jerusalem's rejection of him, as he could see where it would lead them, there was never any question of forcing a relationship upon them.

Instead, he turned his attention to the considerable number of Jews who *did* receive him, knowing that his rejection by the majority of Jews would drive the minority who did accept him to cast the net wider. They would break out of the chrysalis of historic Judaism into the butterfly of God's wider people, those who were willingly gathered from every nation in the world. This issue we looked at in Chapter 6 of this study, especially in sections 4 and 5. The important point for our study of the new heavens and earth is that the New Jerusalem is a description of *all* God's willing people, including the Jewish ones. There are biblical passages which suggest that there will be a time when Jews in far greater numbers will recognise Christ as their expected Messiah, after the full number of non-Jews has been gathered in (see Romans 11:25+ff), but the New Jerusalem is always portrayed as a place for all nations.

The climax of the vision of John, the author of the book of Revelation, consisted of a dazzling description of the New Jerusalem which needed no temple at its heart, because God himself and Christ were there in the middle of it.

3. Task/Question (Group)

Make a study of Revelation 21, especially verses 10-27. You might like to recollect some fictional versions of this city, such as Bunyan's 'Celestial City' in *Pilgrim's Progress*, or even — in certain limited ways — The Emerald City in *The Wizard of Oz*. Why would the author of Revelation list all the precious stones that went into the building of the city? What might he wish to demonstrate? Zechariah 9:16-17 may be helpful.

*

Section 4

What becomes clear, as we look at the various ways the new heaven and the new earth are described by the different biblical authors, is that they really are beyond description. In several of his letters, the Apostle Paul indicates as much, for example in 1 Corinthians 2:9, he says — quoting Isaiah — :

'No eye has seen,
 no ear has heard,
 no mind has conceived
 what God has prepared for those who love him.' (*NIV*)

He then goes on to say that, nevertheless, God has shown it to us by his Spirit. This is a very important point when we are considering these things. We need to be given spiritual insight in order to apprehend them. Otherwise they will seem like nonsense to us, because God's ways are so much higher than our own. Other parts of 1 Corinthians re-emphasise this point, for example the end of the famous chapter 13, verses 9–13 reads:

137

'We know only a portion of the truth, and what we say about God is always incomplete. But when the Complete arrives, our incompletes will be cancelled.

When I was an infant at my mother's breast, I gurgled and cooed like any infant. When I grew up, I left those infant ways for good.

We don't yet see things clearly. We're squinting through a fog, peering through a mist. But it won't be long before the weather clears and the sun shines bright! We'll see it all then, see it all as clearly as God sees us, knowing him directly just as he knows us.

But for right now, until that completeness, we have three things to do to lead us toward that consummation: Trust steadily in God, hope unswervingly, love extravagantly. And the best of the three is love.' (*The Message*)

Jesus suggested this process of gradually — and in fact sometimes suddenly — unfolding revelation when he told his followers:

'I have much more to say to you, more than you can now bear. But when he, the Spirit of truth, comes, he will guide you into all truth. He will not speak on his own: he will speak only what he hears, and *he will tell you what is yet to come.*'
(John 16:12–13 *NIV* italics mine)

This continuing revelation by the Holy Spirit is what gives life to our understanding of the things of God. It is a growing process to which we are called to be attentive and faithful — not trying to anticipate exactly what it means or trying to control the vision of the new heaven and the new earth, but keeping the clues we *are* given until their meaning unfolds, rather in the way that Mary, the mother of Jesus treasured up all the prophecies about him that were given at his birth.

4. Task/Question (By yourself/Group)

Read Luke 2:19 which describes Mary's way of dealing with the astounding prophecies she had been given about her son Jesus — such as Luke 1:32-33, 42 and what the shepherds had told her in Luke 2:11-12. Devise a way in which you could treasure up the prophecies about the new heaven and the new earth. Perhaps you could make use of your answers to the questions in this section so far.

*

Section 5

To expand our picture of the new heaven and the new earth, let us return to the last chapter of Revelation. This final book of the Bible is an account of a vision seen by John of Patmos, who may or may not be the same as John the Beloved Disciple. He wrote down the vision — possibly around 90 AD — along with various messages to different churches in Asia — modern Turkey — for which he seems to have had some pastoral responsibility. Many of these churches were experiencing terrible persecution at the time and John himself had been banished to Patmos because of his Christian faith.

In such hard times at that period of history, writers of religious texts would sometimes write apocalyptic material, in which the great cosmic struggles between good and evil were presented in symbolic terms in an attempt to look beyond the immediate troubles to the overall meaning of what was happening. They were written to encourage hope and confidence in God's sovereignty, and were not meant to be used as timetables for the end of the world, still less as literal accounts of events. Any such attempts reveal a lack of understanding of the literary genre of apocalyptic and have resulted in confused and often damaging meddling in Middle Eastern affairs.

Let us rather approach this apocalyptic text with the humility of Mary and read its messages with imagination and faith, allowing our picture of the future to be informed by the Spirit of God. We have already made a brief study of the 21st chapter of Revelation in connection with the image of the Holy City. In the 22nd chapter of the book, which is also the last chapter of the whole Bible, we find interesting developments of this image.

One is the description of the river flowing from the throne of God right down the middle of the main street of the city. The river consists of the water of life and anyone who is thirsty is urged to drink freely from it (see chapter 21:6) It also waters trees on either side of it which bear regular fruit and leaves and are identified as the tree of life. We have already come across these images earlier in our study and so can identify the water as a reference to the Holy Spirit of God who takes God's life, power, gifts and truth and makes them real and effective in his people.

The fact that the river flows constantly from God's throne and is available to anyone who is thirsty — in fact the thirsty are urged to drink from it — is a reflection of God's abundant, overflowing life, which is constantly poured out for his people. The tree of life refers back to the imagery of Eden, but here, the fruit is freely available, not guarded by angels. It also refers to the body of Christ, given on the 'tree' of the cross and broken to feed his people. The fruit of the tree of life growing in the New Jerusalem may be picked and eaten in order to secure and nourish eternal life. As nothing impure has been allowed into the city, (see chapter 21:27) eternal life can now be a blessing rather than a curse.

5. Task/Question (By yourself)

Add to your pictures of the new heaven and the new earth in the light of this section of our study.

*

Section 6

An interesting detail of the description of the tree of life occurs at the end of verse 2: 'And the leaves of the tree are for the healing of the nations.' The term 'nations' in the biblical texts is often used to mean the non-Jewish or Gentile nations: for example, in Isaiah 55: 5, the prophet addresses his own countrymen in these terms:

> 'You'll summon nations you've never heard of,
> and nations who've never heard of you
>   will come running to you
> Because of me, your God,
>   because The Holy of Israel has honoured you.' (*The Message*)

and in chapter 56: 6-7 we find these words:

> 'And as for the outsiders who now follow me,
>   working for me, loving my name,
>   and wanting to be my servants —
> All who keep Sabbath and don't defile it,
>   holding fast to my covenant —
> I'll bring them to my holy mountain
>   and give them joy in my house of prayer.
> They'll be welcome to worship the same as the 'insiders'
>   to bring burnt offerings and sacrifices to my altar.
> Oh yes, my house of worship
>   will be known as a house of prayer for all people.'

It is also significant that Jesus' greatest anger in his day was directed against the exclusiveness of Judaism — as well as the commercialisation of their religion — when he furiously whipped the wheelers and dealers out of the Temple court where non-Jews were supposed to have peace to worship God. His famous words on that occasion make the point:

'Is it not written: 'My house will be called a house of prayer for all nations'? But you have made it a den of robbers.' (Mark 11:17 *NIV*)

At this stage, the involvement of Gentiles was seen by most Jews as a rather limited affair. If there were Gentiles who wanted in effect to 'become Jews', to undergo circumcision and embrace the Jewish law, they were also to be welcomed into the worship of Judaism as proselytes.

The life, death and resurrection of Jesus marked a watershed which moved the whole salvation story out of traditional Judaism onto the world stage, though never denying its root in Judaism. This was enormously difficult for those who had been brought up within Judaism. This is evident from the story of Peter being called to the house of the Gentile Cornelius, recorded in the New Testament book of The Acts of the Apostles, chapters 10 and 11, and is a wonderful example of the continuing revelation of God's truth by the Holy Spirit.

6. Task/Question (Group/By yourself)

Read this story in Acts 10 and 11 as well as chapter 15, the account of how the early church dealt with the repercussions within the Jewish branch of the church. Is there an issue which you feel has the same potential either for splitting the church today or for inspiring development in the church's understanding of God's will?

Section 7

In the Cornelius story, the key words obviously are:

'Do not call anything impure that God has made clean.'
(Acts 10:15 *NIV*)

This is a very interesting command as it suggests that there had been a time when the animals — and by implication the people — referred to *had* been unclean. In its history the Jewish nation had needed to keep itself untainted by contact with neighbouring peoples so that it would not lose its distinctiveness as the carrier of God's promise to the world.

The worship of Yahweh, for example, was not to be polluted by the worship of other 'gods' which involved such corrupt practices as shrine prostitution or child sacrifice. Elaborate systems of law had been built up to prevent such an outcome and they had solidified into very powerful taboos against any mixing with Gentiles. In the minds of many religious Jews, the original reasons for the prohibitions had been completely forgotten and all that was left was a profound sense of fastidiousness in any dealings with Gentiles.

According to the orthodox Christian understanding of the impact of Christ's life, death and resurrection, the time had now come for the Gentiles or 'the nations' to be brought into the centre of the picture, and for the prophecies of Isaiah and others to begin their fulfilment. The taboos against Gentiles therefore, had to be broken down. As well as providing the promised wholeness for Israel, the work of Christ had made it possible for the Gentiles to be 'clean' without having to go through the ritual of circumcision and without having to take on the whole burden of the Jewish law. 'The nations' were to begin their journey to the New Jerusalem. A section of one of the prophecies already quoted reads:

> 'I'll pour robust well-being into her like a river,
> the glory of nations like a river in flood.'
> (Isaiah 66:12a *The Message*)

The writer of Revelation picks up on this point in chapter 21:24-27:

> 'The nations will walk in (the city's) light and earth's kings bring in their splendour. Its gates will never be shut by day, and there won't be any night. They'll bring the glory and honour of the nations into the City. Nothing dirty or defiled will get into the City, and no one who defiles or deceives. Only those whose names are written in the Lamb's Book of Life will get in.'
> (*The Message*, bracket mine)

Is this the significance of our statement that the leaves of the tree of life are for the healing of the nations? What was impure, God has made clean. Jesus resisted the temptation to win the nations of the world by worshipping Satan, according to the story about his testing which we studied. He would not win them by disobeying God. He would win them by giving up his life for them, so making them clean.

What wonderful news this is — especially for those who love to study the history of the world's great civilisations or for those who love to travel and experience the richness and variety of other cultures. People from all these civilisations and cultures who have been cleaned of all the filth associated with them will stream into the Holy City. Great civilisations that were built on the back of cruel slavery or serfdom will be cleaned of the stain so incurred. Beautiful and vibrant cultures will be represented without the dark underbelly of poverty and corruption which accompany them in our experience.

7. Task/Question (By yourself)

Think of one such civilisation or culture that you have an interest in or experience of. Spend some time considering its strengths and weaknesses. Envisage it in its cleansed state, its strengths flourishing more because of the absence of weaknesses, the unhealthy or exploitative relationships restored to wholeness and the people reconciled. Imagine this as part of the fabulous wealth and variety of the New Jerusalem.

*

Section 8

Let us now try to approach the very heart of the new heaven and the new earth which we have been trying to imagine with all the inadequate images and pictures given to us by the different authors of the Bible and sometimes by artists of various kinds. The essential point about all these pictures and ideas is that they depict a 'place' or perhaps we could call it 'a state of being' where nothing interferes with, and everything contributes to, the wonderful communion between God himself and all those who love him.

Some words from the letter to the Hebrews, chapter 12:22-24, indicate that it will be a vast and varied gathering:

> 'You have come to Mount Zion, to the heavenly Jerusalem, the city of the living God. You have come to thousands upon thousands of angels in joyful assembly, to the church of the firstborn, whose names are written in heaven. You have come to God, the judge of all men, to the spirits of righteous men made perfect, to Jesus the mediator of a new covenant.'

Let us recall some of the key phrases from the passages we have been studying which focus on the exchange of love between God and his people.(I will list the references at the end in order not to interrupt the cumulative effect of considering all these amazing passages together.)

'The earth will be full of the knowledge of the Lord as the waters cover the sea.'

'God will wipe the tears from every face.'

'I'll bring (the outsiders) to my holy mountain and give them joy in my house of prayer.'

'Let us rejoice and be glad and give him glory! For the wedding of the Lamb has come, and his bride has made herself ready.'

'I'll take joy in Jerusalem, take delight in my people.'

'As a mother comforts her child, so I'll comfort you. You will be comforted in Jerusalem.'

'How often I have longed to gather your children together.'

'Now the dwelling of God is with men, and he will live with them. They will be his people and God himself will be with them and be their God.'

'We'll see it all then, see it all as clearly as God sees us, knowing him directly just as he knows us.'

'I did not see a temple in the city, because the Lord God Almighty and the Lamb are its temple. The city does not need the sun or moon to shine on it, for the glory of God gives it light, and the Lamb is its lamp.'

'They will see his face, and his name will be on their foreheads.'
'I, Jesus, sent my Angel to testify to these things for the churches.
I'm the Root and Branch of David, the Bright Morning Star.
'Come!' say the Spirit and the Bride.
Whoever hears, echo, 'Come!'
All who will, come and drink,
Drink freely of the Water of Life!'

(Isaiah 11:9 *NIV*; Isaiah 25:8 *The Message*; Isaiah 56:7 *The Message*; Revelation 19:7 *NIV*; Isaiah 65:19 *The Message*; Isaiah 66:13 *The Message*; Luke 13:34 *NIV*; Revelation 21:3 *NIV*; 1 Corinthians 13:12 *The Message*; Revelation 21:22-23 *NIV*; Revelation 22:4 *NIV*; Revelation 22:16-17 *The Message*.)

Our human experiences which comes closest to this great consummation would probably be those in which we are reconciled to a very dear parent, child, sibling, lover, friend or spouse after a long separation or estrangement; times characterised by overwhelming relief and joy and ones for which the words: 'At last!' most accurately express our feelings.

8. Task/Question (By yourself)

Think of a time in your own story when some such event took place. Add it to your picture of the new heaven and the new earth in whatever way suggests itself to you. Perhaps some of your nearest and dearest have already died and your picture of the new heaven and the new earth may be enriched by imagining them there, made new and in the prime of life. Use photos if you wish.

*

Section 9

Because there is such a biblical emphasis on every nation bringing its best to the New Jerusalem, it is surely both legitimate and to be desired that every culture should have its own characteristic descriptions of the new heaven and the new earth. For example, there is a delightful Gaelic poem entitled: *Theid mi null* (*I will go*) by Donald John MacDonald of South Uist, which describes paradise in terms of the greatest beauty he has experienced in his own island. In translation it reads:

> I will go, so I hope,
> I will go, over the sea
> To the land of the high bens,
> Land of sheldrake and swan;
> I will go, so I hope.
>
> I'll find health there without want,
> I'll find peace in the glens,
> I'll find friendship and love
> And find freedom from ills.
>
> I'll see machairs in bloom,
> I'll see white sandy beaches,
> I'll see a bee on each flower
> Seeking honey for the comb.

I'll have the clean smell of the hay,
So wholesome to my senses,
I'll see bells on the heather
Out on the slopes of the glens.

I'll see dew on the rose
In the youth of the morning,
I'll see the sun make it sparkle,
Shining like diamonds.'

Even in translation, the longing and beauty in this poem come across powerfully, and hint at the richness at the heart of this particular culture as well as the characteristic loveliness of this particular landscape.

The opening two stanzas of another song by this poet provide us with two more images of the new heaven and the new earth in terms appropriate to a community that have depended traditionally on crofting and fishing. It is the song: *Do lamh a Chriosda* (*Your hand O Jesus*). In translation it reads:

'Your hand, O Jesus, be always with us,
Our early planting and roses tending;
Yours be our harvest, our store of barley –
To your barns take us at this life's ending.

You are, in spring time, our dew and fragrance,
A strong, safe harbour, when winds are crying,
Our fruitful fishing, our food, our plenty;
In your nets take us when we are dying. (Italics mine)

In order to build our picture of the new heaven and the new earth we may need to turn more and more to artists of various kinds; musicians, song-writers, poets, painters, even film-makers, to find something which has the same spirit about it. Such artists can have something of the role of prophets in our culture, pointing to what we have forgotten, reminding us of what we do not yet understand.

9. Task/Question (By yourself)

Add to your picture of the new heaven and the new earth by collecting any song words, poems or other works of art you think are true to the spirit of the picture created by biblical writers. Perhaps you are familiar with such works from another country or culture, in which case you might like to enrich your picture with them.

*

Section 10

One final element to include in this present exercise of faith and imagination — although it is of course unlimited in scope — might be what the Hebrews passage quoted above in Section 8 calls, 'the spirits of righteous men made perfect'. This opens up another enormous treasure trove. We have the whole of human history to choose from: any person of integrity, generosity of heart, greatness of vision, who made a beneficial difference to the people around him or her in great or small ways, can be included.

Along with the all-encompassing presence of God himself, any of our own nearest and dearest who have wanted to be near him, and the great company of those who have taken advantage of God's mercy to push their way into the joyful gathering, we have those from every age and nation who have glimpsed enough of God's ways to reflect them to some degree — whether they knew they were doing so or not — their limitations overcome at last.

Because our clichéd pictures of heaven have tended to be so boring and static, we need to realise that they are faulty to some extent. We need to visualise a 'place' or 'state of being' that is vibrant, exciting, dynamic, always unfolding in more and more glorious manifestations. We need to think of it as incorporating growth and development, but without the pain which attends these things in our present incarnation. Obviously, such a state of affairs strains our powers of imagination. All we can do is to rest in our statement of faith that 'God is light and in him is no darkness at all.'

An image which may help us in this respect is that of a young child or toddler exploring his or her surroundings in this world we know. Such a picture gives us delight only when we feel that the child is safe from harm or hurt. Imagine a child experiencing, for example, a sneeze for the first time and the expression of comic astonishment which might appear on his or her face. In Isaiah's picture of the lion lying down with the lamb, the child is safe even if he happens to touch a scorpion's nest, because the scorpion will not sting him. Once the fear of harm is removed, there can be nothing but interest, amusement, excitement, fascination, wonder. Perhaps those who have only just arrived in the new heaven and the new earth will be like infants exploring their new surroundings. Perhaps part of the delight of those who have been there longer will be in welcoming these babes into their new setting.

Imagine an opportunity to experience the growth and development of a baby into a toddler and then into a 'grown up' child without the griefs and tragedies we know in this life. Imagine such a development attended by wise and loving friends, parents, siblings, where all hurts we experienced as children are healed and replaced by what should have happened to ensure the sound establishment of confident trust in the child.

Even more exciting, imagine what maturity might look like in such a setting, where huge varieties of imaginative goodness are multiplied beyond all that can be achieved in our present experience. We could turn on its head the famous opening sentence of Tolstoy's *Anna Karenina*, which reads:

> 'All happy families resemble one another, each unhappy family is unhappy in its own way.'

Just as in the kingdom of God, the last shall be first and the first last, harmony rather than disharmony, will be the most interesting and varied state.

10. Task/Question (By yourself)

People your picture of the new heaven and the new earth with your choice of historical characters who have contributed to the wellbeing of others in ways you find most admirable and/or write a description, story, song or poem in which you explore the possibilities of an unfolding life which is free from harm. Martin Luther King's famous 'I have a dream' speech may give you ideas.

Chapter 10: Return of the Beloved

Section 1

As we come to the last chapter of our study, it may be the time to ask about the transition from this present life — in which we can experience a foretaste of the new heaven and the new earth — to the future, full realisation of these 'Intimations of Immortality' as Wordsworth calls them in his poem of that name. He associates them with early childhood as he imagines that children are still near to the God who created them:

> '... trailing clouds of glory do we come
> From God, who is our home:
> Heaven lies about us in our infancy!'

He goes on to give thanks for:

> '... those first affections,
> Those shadowy recollections,
> Which, be they what they may,
> Are yet the fountain-light of all our day,
>   [... ...] truths that wake,
> To perish never.'

Wordsworth laments the fading of the glory of childhood, but he maintains that the vision we had then is truer than the more mundane view of the world which replaces it in adult life, and believes that the childhood vision should continue to inform our understanding of our lives and our surroundings.

A question we may ask is: do we move to the fully realised experience of the new heaven and the new earth by gradual evolution and progress, or is there to be a complete cut-off point in this present experience of reality when a new order breaks into it? If we are to maintain unbreakable hope, this is a vital question, both for our expectation of what will happen to the whole cosmos, and for what will happen to us as individuals.

The biblical answer to this question seems again and again to be that there will be a radical change of everything, which will happen suddenly and unexpectedly. A useful passage in this connection is to be found in Paul's first letter to the Corinthians in chapter 15. We have looked at this chapter in connection with the resurrection already, but in verses 50-56, we read:

> 'I need to emphasise, friends, that our natural, earthly lives don't in themselves lead us by their very nature into the kingdom of God. Their very 'nature' is to die, so how could they 'naturally' end up in the Life kingdom?'
>
> But let me tell you something wonderful, a mystery I'll probably never fully understand. We're not all going to die — *but* we are all going to be changed. You hear a blast to end all blasts from a trumpet, and in the time that you look up and blink your eyes — it's over. On signal from that trumpet from heaven, the dead will be up and out of their graves, beyond the reach of death, never to die again. At the same moment and in the same way, we'll all be changed. In the resurrection scheme of things, this has to happen: everything perishable taken off the shelves and replaced by the imperishable, this mortal replaced by the immortal. Then the saying will come true:
> 'Death swallowed by triumphant Life!
> Who got the last word, oh, Death?
> Oh, Death, who's afraid of you now?'
> It was sin that made death so frightening and law-code guilt that gave sin its leverage, its destructive power. But now in a single victorious stroke of Life, all three — sin, guilt, death — are gone, the gift of our Master, Jesus Christ. Thank God!' (*The Message*)

Here Paul spells out that this will be no 'ordinary' cataclysm because it will result in all the dead being raised and all the living being radically changed into immortal beings at a stroke. He also admits that it is a mystery that has been revealed to him which he does not fully understand.

1. Task/Question (By yourself/Group)

Try to imagine such an event happening. An effort of this kind can cause us to feel afraid, but if Paul is right about this, we will be freed from fear at last, because fear has to do with a perception of danger to our lives, and they will no longer be subject to death, hence the quoted taunt to 'Death', which will no longer hold that sort of power over us. The gun with which we have been threatened all these years will be revealed as having no bullets in it after all.

Section 2

The central element of this sudden and radical change in everything we know is described again and again by the different biblical authors as the return of Jesus Christ, the person believed by many to be the expected Jewish Messiah and the Saviour of all people, both Jewish and Gentile, as well as the whole created universe. This return, for example, is referred to by the writers of the gospels, who report many of Jesus' own words on the subject. We looked at some of them in Chapter 8, Section 6 of this study, from Matthew 24:30, so let us look at some of Christ's words about himself from Luke's account.

As in Matthew, the mention of Christ's return comes after a grim list of the tragedies of routine world history, with which we are only too familiar because of the daily news bulletins brought to us by the media. There will also be massive disturbances in the cosmos, an indication of which is also given to us by the predictions of scientists. We need to know that these things were bound to happen, given the resistance to God's ways which abounds in our world. The return of Christ brings all this to a halt as Luke records it in Jesus' own words:

> 'It will seem like all hell has broken loose — sun, moon, stars, earth, sea, in an uproar and everyone all over the world in a panic, the wind knocked out of them by the threat of doom, the powers-that-be quaking.
> And then — then — they'll see the Son of Man welcomed in grand style — a glorious welcome! When all this starts to happen, up on your feet. Stand tall with your heads high. Help is on the way!' (Luke 21:25-28 *The Message*)

Then in John's gospel there are the reassuring words we have come back to several times in this study, from chapter14:1-3:

> 'Do not let your hearts be troubled. Trust in God: trust also in me. In my Father's house are many rooms; if it were not so, I would have told you. I am going there to prepare a place for you. And if I go and prepare a place for you, *I will come back* and take you to be with me that you also may be where I am.' (*NIV* Italics mine)

Luke continues his account in Acts and in the first chapter we read the account of the last time the disciples saw Jesus in the flesh and on this occasion, an angelic voice tells them of Jesus' return:

'When they were together for the last time they asked, 'Master, are you going to restore the kingdom to Israel now? Is this the time?'

He told them, 'You don't get to know the time. Timing is the Father's business. What you'll get is the Holy Spirit. And when the Holy Spirit comes on you, you will be able to be my witnesses in Jerusalem, all over Judea and Samaria, even to the ends of the world.'

These were his last words. As they watched, he was taken up and disappeared in a cloud. They stood there, staring into the empty sky. Suddenly two men appeared — in white robes! They said, 'You Galileans! — why do you just stand here looking up at an empty sky? This very Jesus who was taken up from among you to heaven will come as certainly — and mysteriously — as he left.' (Verses 6-11 *The Message*)

2. Task/Question (Group)

Look again at the Matthew account of this event — chapter 24, verses 30-31. In *The Message* it reads:

'Then, the Arrival of the Son of Man! It will fill the skies — no one will miss it. Unready people all over the world, outsiders to the splendour and power, will raise a huge lament as they watch the Son of Man blazing out of heaven. At that same moment, he'll dispatch his angels with a trumpet blast summons, pulling in God's chosen from the four winds, from pole to pole.'

In this extract, the emphasis is on lament rather than celebration. Why would this be so?

*

Section 3

You will no doubt have concluded that the lament is to be raised by those who are unready. They will have decided that nothing much is ever going to change, that the gross injustices they are perpetrating or ignoring can continue undisturbed, that they will never be called to account, that they have 'got away with it'. The prospect of Jesus' return should have this sobering effect upon us all, focussing the mind wonderfully on whether or not we are ready to meet him.

A childish comparison may clarify this issue for us: when the teacher is called out of the room for a while and the pupils are left to get on with their work, some will do so, some will laze about doing nothing, while still others will start looking for ways of causing trouble by bothering their classmates or destroying the environment. If the teacher comes back unexpectedly, the last two groups will 'raise a huge lament' as they have been caught red-handed and their work is not done. They can expect to be called to account for their failures and the workers can expect to hear the teacher's 'Well done!'

Many of Jesus' parables told similar stories of warning and encouragement. What this means for our study of unbreakable hope is that such a hope is rigorous and does not allow for complacency or deliberate wickedness. Rather it encourages us to make our best efforts in what we have been given to do, as the results will be very significant for ourselves and other people and in some cases for the environment too.

Some of the letters of the New Testament also refer in some detail to Jesus' promised return. Both the first and the second letters of Paul to the Thessalonian church, for example, contain significant material on the subject. The first such passage is in the context of Paul urging them to moderate their grief about those of Christ's followers who have already died, or 'fallen asleep' as Paul puts it:

> 'Brothers, we do not want you to be ignorant about those who fall asleep, or to grieve like the rest of men, who have no hope. We believe that Jesus died and rose again and so we believe that God will bring with Jesus those who have fallen asleep in him. According to the Lord's own word, we tell you that we who are still alive, who are left till the coming of the Lord, will certainly not precede those who have fallen asleep. For the Lord himself will come down from heaven, with a loud command, with the voice of the archangel and with the trumpet call of God, and the dead in Christ will rise first.
>
> After that, we who are still alive and are left will be caught up together with them in the clouds to meet the Lord in the air. And so we will be with the Lord for ever. Therefore encourage each other with these words.
>
> Now, brothers, about times and dates we do not need to write to you, for you know very well that the day of the Lord will come like a thief in the night. While people are saying, 'Peace and safety', destruction will come on them suddenly, as labour pains on a pregnant woman, and they will not escape.'
> (1 Thessalonians 4:13-5:3 *NIV*)

Again we find this mixture of encouragement and warning about the future return of Christ. Because the time of this event is unknown, there is a constant need to be ready.

3. Task/Question (Group)

Look up the references to this event in 2 Thessalonians 1:6-7 and 2:8. What aspects of the return of Christ as described here suggest that it will be an event seen by everyone?

*

Section 4

In both these passages from 2 Thessalonians, Jesus' return is described in terms of a spectacular and conclusive victory over all that is evil. It also seems that evil will have escalated to unprecedented levels prior to his return, and that he will put an abrupt and thorough stop to it.

In many passages of the Bible, we are warned about this increase in wickedness which will take place and yet somehow we are always shocked when we hear of some new outrage. There is something good about never getting used to what the Bible calls 'the mystery of iniquity' (2 Thessalonians 2:7 *AV*) as it is only right and proper that our whole selves should rebel against evil, yet we must be aware that there will be this increase of wickedness, so that we do not lose our grasp on unbreakable hope in the face of it.

This event is also referred to by the author of the second letter attributed to Peter, the disciple, apostle and leader in the early church:

> 'First of all you must understand that in the last days scoffers will come, scoffing and following their own evil desires. They will say, 'Where is this 'coming' he promised? Ever since our fathers died, everything goes on since the beginning of creation,' But they deliberately forget that long ago by God's word the heavens existed and the earth was formed out of water and by water. By these waters also the world of that time was deluged and destroyed. By the same word the present heavens and earth are reserved for fire, being kept for the day of judgment and destruction of ungodly men.......But the day of the Lord will come like a thief. The heavens will disappear with a roar: the elements will be destroyed by fire, and the earth and everything in it will be laid bare...... That day will bring about the destruction of the heavens by fire, and the elements will melt in the heat.'
> (2 Peter 3:3-7, 10 +12b-13 *NIV*)

We looked at parts of this passage in Chapter 8, Section 5 of our study when considering the issue of the judgment of God — more particularly his patience in holding back the end of all things in order to give everyone a chance to be ready. (2 Peter 3:9+15) In the context of Jesus' return, the element of fire is regularly referred to. It sounds very like a literal conflagration of the whole cosmos in which everything perishable will be burned up leaving only the imperishable new creation, which had its beginning in the earthly life of Jesus, and which has been secretly growing ever since.

4. Task/Question (Group)

Does it sound possible scientifically — that all we know of our universe could go up in flames? Suggest a few scenarios of how this might happen.

*

Section 5

Of course we have to admit that we do not know exactly how these changes described in our biblical prophecies will come about — and I am not forgetting that some doing this study may still have reservations about the authority of scripture in any case. Even so, what we know of possible futures for the earth from science does not preclude the burning up of everything. I'm sure you will have considered some sort of speed up of global warming as a possible scenario. I'm sure you will have considered a nuclear holocaust of some description. There has even been recent scientific speculation — reported in *The New Scientist* early in 2008 — that a 'rogue' bubble universe could rush into our universe and obliterate it before we could blink. Our own sun is set to expand into a 'Red Giant', consuming all the inner planets, including the earth — although human life may be extinct by that time. The point is we have messages from scientific sources that are comparable to the biblical prophecies.

There is no doubt that thinking about these issues can be quite terrifying unless we have a secure grasp of another of our Christian doctrines: the sovereignty of God, or to put it in a more accessible form:

'He's got the whole world in his hands'

as the children's hymn has it. In Jesus' words, this becomes — as we have read in John 14:1:

'Do not let your hearts be troubled. Trust in God; trust also in me.' (*NIV*)

These three commands are our only — but our unbreakable — way of being able to contemplate the return of Christ. Because we do not know when or how the 'Day of the Lord' will come, we can rest in God's control of the whole issue, focussing our attention, as he encouraged us to do, on being ready: that is, by committing ourselves to obeying the commands he has given us. So what are these commands that are repeated so often in connection with Jesus' return?

The first is the one we have just been considering: that is, *not to be alarmed* when we consider the way world history is going, *not to be worried* about what we shall say if we are questioned in a hostile way about our faith, but to trust God — Father, Son and Holy Spirit. When Jesus was asked what work God requires of us, he answered:

'The work of God is this: *to believe in the one he has sent.*'
(John 6:29 *NIV* italics mine.)

These are commands to be obeyed — work to be done. It is rigorous and requires effort. Whenever we feel afraid, we are commanded to put aside our fear and replace it with trust; not any old gullible or mindless trust, but trust in the God in whom there is no darkness at all. The more we know about him — and in fact, the more we know him personally — the more we will be able to put our trust in him; the more we practise putting our trust in him, the more we will find him to be trustworthy. Eventually we will be able to look horror in the face and still trust because Jesus has done it before us. At the most awful moment of his suffering, when he felt abandoned, denied and betrayed by God and man, Jesus said:

'Father, into your hands I commit my spirit.' (Luke 23:46 *NIV*)

or, in another translation:

'Father, I place my life in your hands!' (*The Message*)

He put himself and all he had done into God's hands, trusting that God would bring about his will. This faith, this restful trust was exercised by Jesus at the moment when all his work looked as if it had ended in a complete and tragic fiasco. We know the sequel: the resurrection, the incredulous joy of the disciples, the energising power of the Holy Spirit to launch the young church on its mission to tell everyone about what had been done for them, the seismic shift in the whole world, beginning in a small corner of the mighty Roman Empire and spreading out to have a great and lasting impact long after Rome was history.

Trust, then is our first and most important task or 'work' as we wait for Jesus' return. Anything else we do must be done in the spirit of this restful trust; otherwise it will turn into stressful and ineffective striving by people who have forgotten that the whole world is in his hands. *He* is the Saviour of the world, not us.

5. Task/Question (Group)

Look up 1 Corinthians 11:23-26 for a God-given way of keeping Christ's saving action central to our lives and to our message until his return.

*

Section 6

Another command we are given again and again in connection with Jesus' return is that we must watch, be ready, be alert and on guard, so that the day does not catch us napping. The restful trust described above does not mean that we are asleep or oblivious to what is going on. Things we must watch out for, or be aware of, are, for example, that there will be fraudulent claims by false 'messiahs' to have the secret of life or the answer to world problems. Anything which suggests that the work of Christ was not really necessary, but that we can be saved by other means is a distraction from the unbreakable hope established by him.

This is not to deny that much can and should be done to improve life through education, politics, social work, charitable effort and so on but these fields of activity tend to focus on the external causes and effects of the problems we face. The inner sickness we all suffer from means that even if we were put into a perfect environment, it would not be long before the problems we are all familiar with would resurface, unresolved. The only surgery radical enough to excise the cancer is to let the patient die with Christ and start again with a new creation in him.

Another way we are to watch that we are not deceived is that people will try to make us believe that the end of the world is coming soon and we will miss it unless we follow them. Jesus assured his listeners that it will be quite clear to all when it happens and that they must not chase after people making special claims to inside information on the subject.

We are also urged to watch that we do not get bogged down with over-indulgence or with the regular anxieties of life and forget about the most important issues. Some people turn this command to watch into a literal staying awake to keep vigil at certain times in the church's year, such as on Christmas Eve or on Maundy Thursday into Good Friday, in order to remember the key events in the life, death and resurrection of Christ. Such occasions help to take the focus away from our own daily concerns and remind us of more important realities.

This leads naturally into a related command: to pray. In fact the two often appear together in the biblical texts: 'Watch and pray'. This is the way to be ready for testing times and was Jesus' instruction to his disciples before the crucifixion. They were unable to keep their eyes open on that occasion and handled themselves badly as a result. The same warning is given by Jesus with regard to his return. In Luke's account, chapter 21, verse 36, he says:

> 'Be always on the watch, and pray that you may be able to escape all that is about to happen, and that you may be able to stand before the Son of Man,' (*NIV*)

In fact prayer, as well as being good preparation for testing times, is also an effective way of banishing anxiety, the issue we considered first of all of the commands connected with looking for Jesus' return. The classic text in this connection is in Philippians 4:4-7:

> 'Celebrate God all day, every day. I mean, revel in him! Make it as clear as you can to all you meet that you're on their side, working with them and not against them. Help them see that the Master is about to arrive. He could show up any minute!
> Don't fret or worry. Instead of worrying, pray. Let petitions and praises shape your worries into prayers, letting God know your concerns. Before you know it, a sense of God's wholeness, everything coming together for good, will come and settle you down. It's wonderful what happens when Christ replaces worry at the centre of your life. (*The Message*)

The prayer described here not only disposes of worries but moves into thanksgiving, praise and rejoicing in God. As we hand over responsibility to him, we reflect on and delight in his ability and willingness to do for us what we cannot do for ourselves. The only appropriate response on our part is to worship him. How could we be anything other than overjoyed at the return of such a person? The discipline of prayer — both requests and thanks — when offered in the spirit of restful trust, prepares us for the return of Christ so that we may see his return as wonderful and amazing rather than terrifying.

6. Task/Question (By yourself)

Choose an issue which is worrying you at the moment. Take some time to lay it all out before God. Write it down if you find that helpful. Thank him for hearing you and for taking responsibility for this worrying matter. When you get up from that prayer, leave the issue in God's hands, refusing to resume your worrying — seventy times a day if need be. Then look out for his answer. It may be simply a change in the way you see the issue; it may be a development in the situation itself; it may be a fresh idea of something you can do to improve things or even unexpected help from someone else. When the answer comes, you will find yourself well able to thank, praise and even worship him.

*

Section 7

The church as a body has also been given commands to obey as part of our preparation for Jesus' return. We have looked in Chapter 3, Section 4 of this study at the commission to bring as many people as possible into the way of following Jesus, to baptise and teach them to change their lives, to receive God's forgiveness and the life of the Holy Spirit within. In other words we have been called to play our part in getting others as well as ourselves ready for his return. We also looked in Chapter 8, Section 5 of our study at the mercy of God in delaying his return so that many more have the opportunity to be ready when he comes, having heard about God's provision for them.

The story of the sheep and the goats — in Matthew 25:31-46 — also considered in Chapter 8, Section 6, provides another indication of what we should be doing as we wait and hope for Jesus' return, and that is to reach out to those in distress and need, treating them with as much care as we would Jesus himself. The fact that those in the story who did help the unfortunate were unaware that they were doing it for Christ himself suggests that some people follow his ways without being fully aware of it. All the same, these compassionate activities make them ready to recognise Christ when he comes, because they are of the same spirit.

As well as making sure that as many people as possible know about Christ and his offer of wholeness, there is the task of caring for those who have already started on the path of following Christ. In one of Jesus' parables recorded by Matthew and Luke, he tells of a master returning home and discovering what his servants have been doing in his absence. Peter, the leader of the disciples, asks if the parable is for the disciples only or for everyone. Jesus' answer seems to have special application to those in leadership positions, because he replies — as he often does — with a question:

> 'Who then is the faithful and wise manager, whom the master puts in charge of his servants to give them their food allowance at the proper time? It will be good for that servant whom the master finds doing so when he returns.' (Luke 12:42-43 *NIV*)

Jesus then goes on to point out that more will be expected of those who have been given positions of responsibility.

This task of caring for the church was given very specifically to Peter in an interesting account at the end of John's gospel, when Jesus appeared after his resurrection to a group of seven of his disciples as they were fishing unsuccessfully on the Sea of Galilee. Jesus directed them where to cast the net and they pulled in a huge and unexpected catch. After eating with them, Jesus walked along the shore and spoke to Peter especially, giving him the opportunity to say three times that he loved Jesus, a painful restoration after Peter's threefold denial of him. After each of Peter's declarations, Jesus gave him a specific task to do, expressing his trust in the one who had proved so untrustworthy in the past:

> 'Feed my lambs.' 'Take care of my sheep.' and 'Feed my sheep.' (John 21: extracts from 15-17 *NIV*)

Jesus told Peter of the kind of death he would meet and repeated his original call to Peter:

> 'Follow me!' (v. 19 *NIV*)

7. Task/Question (Group)

Read on in John 21:20-24 for an example of how false rumours about Jesus' return could start.

*

Section 8

In several of the New Testament letters, there appear lists of gifts God has given to his people for the work he has called them to do. Just as the actual jobs we do vary tremendously — we considered that variety in Chapter 3, Section 1 of this study — so do our God-given aptitudes. For these gifts to reveal the God who gave them, they have to be exercised in the spirit of love. An example which brings out the right and wrong use of gifts is found in Paul's letter to the Romans 12:6-8:

> 'If you preach, just preach God's message, nothing else: if you help, just help, don't take over; if you teach, stick to your teaching; if you give encouraging guidance, be careful that you don't get bossy; if you're put in charge, don't manipulate; if you're called to give aid to people in distress, keep your eyes open and be quick to respond; if you work with the disadvantaged, don't let yourself get irritated with them or depressed by them. Keep a smile on your face.' (*The Message*)

It is clear from this list that some of the gifts will be exercised within the church and some in the community, but even those exercised within the church are for the purpose of equipping the church members for their work in the community as one of the other lists makes clear:

> 'It was (Christ) who gave some to be apostles, some to be prophets, some to be evangelists, and some to be pastors and teachers, to prepare God's people for works of service.' (Ephesians 4:11-12a *NIV*)

This does not mean necessarily that there will be formal lessons in churches about how to evangelise or help the needy or whatever, although such may sometimes be useful. Rather it means that the love and faith of the members will be built up so that they themselves will be instructed by the Holy Spirit in how they may best follow the way of Christ in their homes and places of work and influence. The keynote in all the lists of gifts is the infinite variety of ways in which the work of Christ can be carried out. What unifies these efforts is the loving spirit in which they are done, not the uniformity of execution.

The point in connection with Jesus' return is that the talents we have been given should be put to use in God's service so that we may give a good account to him when he comes. The very word 'talent' comes from the parable we looked at from Matthew 25:14-30 at the end of Section 6 in Chapter 8 of this study. A talent was originally an amount of money, but in a significant semantic shift, it has come to mean any gift or ability we have been given and which should be put to good use. It is worth noting that the praise given by the master to the one who turned two talents into four is exactly the same as that given to the one who turned five talents into ten. The fact that they had different amounts to begin with determined how much they were able to do. The praise is because they used what they had been given. They were not compared favourably or otherwise with one another.

8. Task/Question (By yourself)
Review your own gifts and talents — including money — as honestly as you can before God. You may need feedback from others to be sure of your analysis. Are you in a position to use them in your home, work, church and in the wider world? If not, make it a matter for prayer and expect an answer.

*

Section 9

Much misery, guilt, dissatisfaction, ineffectiveness and frustration can arise if we have a fixed or rigid view of what our true role is in any given situation. We may, without fully realising it, be working to someone else's agenda, trying to fulfil our parents' dreams, for example, or executing an outdated church programme that may have been right twenty years ago. Our view of what is required of us may be stale and unimaginative. Old baggage may need to be cleared away.

Patient attention to the still, small voice will bring release and joy and a certainty about our path in following Christ, both individually and as a body. This vision must be carefully guarded as it will be encroached upon by all sorts of other tasks that sound plausible as the right way to go, but will in practice take attention, resources, time and energy away from our true calling and endanger our ability to complete the task we have been given. That said, something that initially presents itself as an interruption, may have in it an essential aspect of our true calling. In other words, we must be alert to the possibilities in our circumstances as well as keeping a steady course.

Even when we are on track in that way, there will be major trials and obstacles for much of the time, but if we know we are following Christ in the path he has chosen for us, we will be more likely to weather storms successfully. A simple little song by Diane Davis expresses this quiet confidence beautifully:

'God has called you, he will not fail you,
God has called you, he will not fail you,
God has called you, he will not fail you,
So trust in God and obey him.

God has called us, we will not fail him,
God has called us, we will not fail him,
God has called us, we will not fail him,
So trust in God and obey him.'
(Published in *Sound of Living Waters*)

Jesus often spoke of the importance of finishing the work the Father had given him, for example, his prayer on the night before he died, recorded by John, includes the words:

'I have brought you glory on earth by completing the work you gave me to do.' (John 17:4 *NIV*)

Then, just before he died, he said:

'It is finished.' (John 19:30 *NIV*)

Jesus was only about thirty-three years old when he died, and his public ministry had only lasted for about three years. Many people would have judged that his work was anything but finished, yet he knew he had done what the Father had given him to do and so he was satisfied.

We need to have this same determination to finish the work each of us has been given to do, be it long or short.

9. Task/Question (Group)
Read 1 Corinthians 15:58 and 2 Timothy 4:6-8 for encouragement in finishing the work you have been given.

*

Section 10

In the second of these passages, Paul tells his younger colleague, Timothy, that he feels he is coming to the end of his life, and that his life's work is done. He does not expect human recognition — in fact he suggests his life will be sacrificed — but he expects his vindication from God himself and he says it will be the same for everyone looking forward to Christ's return.

One of the hardest situations in which to maintain hope is when what we see as our God-given work is unappreciated, ignored or even despised by other people, especially those we admire or from whom we might have expected understanding. This can be a tricky area, because it is of course quite in order for those who love us and who are committed to us to challenge aspects of what we are doing or to point out anything we seem to have overlooked or need to take account of. It is easier — but can still be quite difficult — to set aside criticism if it is offered in a hostile way by those who do not have any relationship with us.

When we experience a discouraging response to our work from friend or foe, we may need to have the humility before God to check out the truth of what has been said or done — or *not* said or done — to see if any part of this unwelcome response needs to be taken on board. We may also need to be healed from the hurt of it by asking directly in prayer ourselves or asking someone else to pray for us. After that, it is a question of waiting until we sense whether the original calling to do the work is still there. Perhaps we will conclude that we were mistaken about the calling in the first place. If this *is* the case, however, it should come as a relief to us. Our thoughts in such a situation should take the form of something like this:

> 'Oh good! I'm not being required to do this after all. Now I can be free to find out what my true work is.'

If, on the other hand, we feel sad and as if robbed of something which is truly ours, then we should return to the original calling and seek our confirmation in it from God himself and from more sympathetic human sources. When this has happened we will be in a stronger position to cope with unfavourable responses in future.

However, we may sometimes be physically prevented by our critics from access to the field of operation in which we have been serving God. If such is the case, we can only 'shake the dust off our feet', as Jesus instructed his disciples when he sent them out with the message of God's kingdom to the towns and villages of Israel. If their offer of peace was refused, he promised that the proffered peace would return to them. Read Matthew 10 for Jesus' instructions about how to handle opposition in your God-given work.

However, being ready for Jesus' return is not just a question of *doing* our God-given work, it is also a question of *being* our God-given selves. In Peter's second letter, he says, after describing the end of all things:

> 'Since everything will be destroyed in this way, what kind of people ought you to be? You ought to live holy and godly lives as you look forward to the day of God and speed its coming......So then, dear friends, since you are looking forward to this, make every effort to be found spotless, blameless and at peace with him.' (2 Peter 3:11-12+14 *NIV*)

This command — to live a holy and godly life — is the only one connected with the return of Christ that suggests that Christ's followers can have any influence at all on when that day comes. Peter suggests they can 'speed its coming' or, as the *Revised Standard Version* has it; 'hastening the coming of the day of God'. Just as evil multiplies and increases, so does goodness and godliness. Two of Jesus' parables suggest this secret growth of goodness:

> 'He told them another parable: 'The kingdom of heaven is like a mustard seed, which a man took and planted in his field. Though it is the smallest of all your seeds, yet when it grows, it is the largest of garden plants and becomes a tree, so that the birds of the air come and perch in its branches.'
> He told them still another parable: 'The kingdom of heaven is like yeast that a woman took and mixed into a large amount of flour until it worked all through the dough." (Matthew 13:31-33 *NIV*)

The writer of Revelation also indicates that there is a parallel development of evil and good towards the end of history:

> 'The Angel continued, 'Don't seal the words of the prophecy of this book; don't put it away on the shelf. Time is just about up. Let evildoers do their worst and the dirty-minded go all out in pollution, but let the righteous maintain a straight course and the holy continue on in holiness.' (Revelation 22: 10-11 *The Message*)

This secret growth of goodness should have a hugely encouraging effect upon our unbreakable hope, because we can be so battered by the bad news and forget that most media people reckon that good news is not worth reporting. Let us become purveyors of good news as well as being good news ourselves by living as our God-given selves. In case this sounds like an impossible task, we must remember that we are not left struggling alone with it. Paul's words at the end of 1 Thessalonians 5: 23-24 are a salutary reminder:

> 'May God himself, the God who makes everything holy and whole, make you holy and whole, put you together — spirit, soul and body — and keep you fit for the coming of our Master, Jesus Christ. The One who called you is completely dependable and he will do it.
> If he said it, he'll do it!' (*The Message*)

This being the case, we can surely feel free to add our prayers to the great cry of all creation described by the author of Revelation, begging Jesus to return and urging everyone who is thirsty for him to be part of the new creation:

> 'Come!' say the Spirit and the Bride.
> Whoever hears, echo, 'Come!'
> Is anyone thirsty? Come!
> All who will, come and drink,
> Drink freely of the Water of Life!' (Revelation 22:17 *The Message*)

10. Task/Question (By yourself)
Can you make this prayer your own?

Notes for Group Leaders

If your group is accustomed to reading, study and discourse, you will usually be able to expect that they will have read the chapter in advance of the group meeting. If they are not in the habit of this kind of activity, some will have done so but may have struggled with it and others will find it too daunting or unfamiliar. In either case it is not possible to study a whole chapter in detail at one meeting of, for example, an hour and a half's duration, because there is too much material. Some of it should be regarded as background reading.

When preparing for the meeting, therefore, it is probably good to select four or five of the key sections of the chapter for detailed study and summarise the rest for your group. Actually reading those sections together may be appropriate for some groups as that either introduces the topic or refreshes the memories of those who have been able to read it in advance. It is also valuable to read together some of the key passages of scripture. Some members of the group will be willing to read aloud but for others it might be quite an ordeal, so make it clear that there is no obligation to read aloud, or indeed to make vocal contribution to discussion. For some people, simply being able to listen to others is enough at first and for some considerable time. Participation will of course also be easier if the size of each group is kept to about a dozen or fewer.

As the questions and tasks at the end of each section are in some cases quite personal, I have indicated which ones may be easier for shared consideration (although note that these may not be the questions at the end of the sections you have chosen as key ones for discussion). However, group members should be given opportunity at a convenient moment to speak about their answers to the individual questions at the end of the other sections if they so desire. They may have spent time thinking about the issues and want to discuss aspects of them.

I have found it beneficial at the beginning of each meeting to summarise the previous week's study and to remind the group of some of the points made by individual group members as this builds up the sense of working together on the project and of learning from each other. Frequently the discussion may lead naturally into prayer, although there will not be time for a full blown prayer meeting as such if the meeting is to be of a manageable length.

If the study is to be undertaken in Lent, the first six chapters would make a suitable study for that period, chapter six focussing especially on Jesus' death and resurrection. There would then be the option of continuing with the last four chapters at a suitable point between Easter and Pentecost if the group so desired.

About the author...

During the course of her life, Margaret Keltie has sought to express the reason for the hope that is in her in various ways.

Well aware of the evangelistic imperative of the church, whether in this country or in the various parts of Africa where she has lived, she has experimented with different ways of communicating Christian truth.

Her main work has been the teaching of English in secondary schools in both Malawi and Scotland. She has been particularly concerned with teaching the skill of understanding the meaning of any writer and of discerning the difference between literal and metaphorical language. She also believes wholeheartedly in the communication of truth by means of story.

This study of hope has afforded her the scope to express her lifelong concern with the accurate communication of the truth of the Christian gospel in contemporary thought patterns for the sake both of those who already believe it and those who are still seeking.

A word from the publisher...

We hope you have enjoyed reading **The Pilgrim's Tale** as much as we have.

Shoving Leopard is a small publisher of books designed to inspire and challenge people on their spiritual journey. The One Hundred Days series will include the following titles among others:

The Penitent's Tale: one hundred days of grace
The Mystic's Tale: one hundred days of love
The Pardoner's Tale: one hundred days of mercy

If you are interested in reading more, or if you feel inspired to contribute to or write a title in the series, please contact us at www.shovingleopard.com for further information.

Lightning Source UK Ltd.
Milton Keynes UK

172368UK00001B/50/P